THE BOY'S BOOK OF HANDICRAFTS

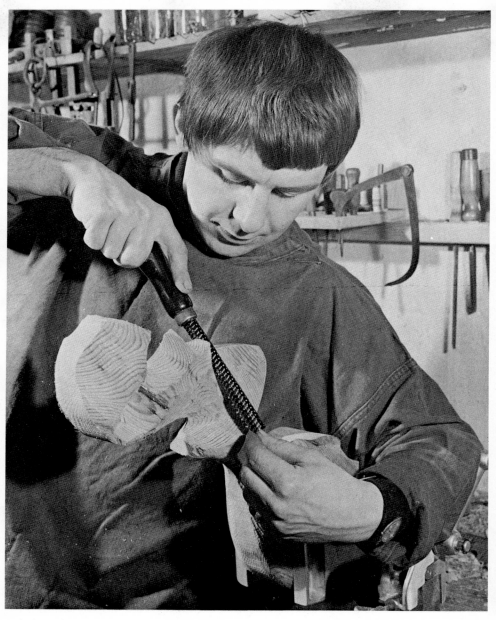

Stanley Works
(Great Britain) Ltd.

Frontispiece: Using a special tool to form an attractive sculpture in grained wood.

THE BOY'S BOOK OF

HANDICRAFTS

Edited by
DAVID SHAW

WARD LOCK LIMITED · LONDON

ISBN 0 7063 1275 9

Ward Lock Limited, 116 Baker Street,
London WIM 2BB

Printed in Spain
by Editorial fher s.a. - Bilbao

EDITOR'S PREFACE

Young men, like every other group of people, have their likes and dislikes. One kind of handicraft may be a pleasure to one boy and a bore to another. In this book I have tried to cater for this by presenting a pretty wide variety of subjects. Some of these, especially the woodworking items, may be considered a bit outside the scope of a boy, but this is not so. At a great number of schools boys are building pieces of furniture which many a cabinet-maker would be proud to call his own.

It is quite impossible in one book to give more than a few examples of a particular craft. However, when you have successfully made these there is no reason why you shouldn't try out your own ideas. This will not only test your technical skill but—equally important—bring out your latent creative abilities.

A few of the subjects, like simple plumbing, may be more 'handyman' than 'handicraft', but they need the same degree of skill and 'knowhow'—and can be just as absorbing. Further, to a hard-pressed parent such skills in a son could mean a great deal, especially at the present time when it is often difficult to get the services of a plumber or electrician.

One final word. Many of the crafts need rather expensive tools so be sure that you really want to do the subject—you could so easily waste a great deal of valuable pocket-money.

CONTENTS

A basic home workshop and tools

In addition to enthusiasm and skill, the handy boy must either possess a tool kit, or have the use of one. (See pages 12 and 13). Besides a tool kit, there is always the problem of where to work. If possible it is best to have part of a garage or a dry, outside shed for a permanent working place.

When your work place has been settled, the next most important thing is a bench to work on. This really is important. Where it is impossible to have a permanent workshop, you will probably have to use the kitchen table. Now, however careful you may be, the surface of a table is bound to suffer. It is a good plan, therefore, to make a portable bench-top as shown in Fig. 1, which can be placed over a table and held in position by

Figure 1. Three types of rigid working benches.

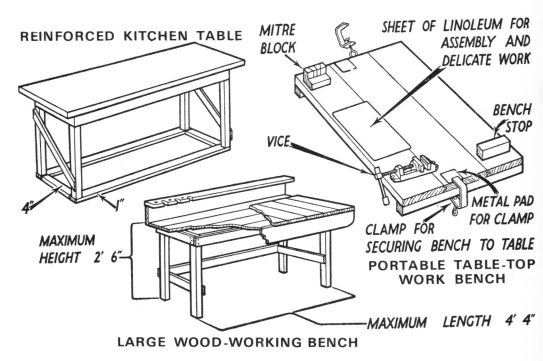

REINFORCED KITCHEN TABLE

MITRE BLOCK

SHEET OF LINOLEUM FOR ASSEMBLY AND DELICATE WORK

BENCH STOP

VICE

4"

1"

MAXIMUM HEIGHT 2' 6"

CLAMP FOR SECURING BENCH TO TABLE

METAL PAD FOR CLAMP

PORTABLE TABLE-TOP WORK BENCH

MAXIMUM LENGTH 4' 4"

LARGE WOOD-WORKING BENCH

two C-clamps. Tongued-and-grooved boards, secured by a cross-strip at each end, will serve for the top.

The ideal, without doubt, is the type of wood-working bench shown in Fig. 1, although the high cost of timber will put it beyond the funds of most boys to build.

If you do decide to build a proper bench, the type chosen will depend on whether your main concern is woodwork or metalwork, since the carpenter's bench differs in some respects from that used by the metal-worker. It is, for example, lower; a maximum height of 2 ft. 6 in. is suitable for an adult, whereas a younger person will need a bench that is shorter if he is to work in comfort. To save the trouble of lengthening the legs as the years go by, a wooden platform to stand on, raised on battens, will enable the young carpenter to work without difficulty.

A satisfactory alternative to the conventional, but expensive, work-bench can easily be made from an old kitchen table. Fig. 1 shows how to make one rigid with lengths of 4 in. by 1 in. timber.

Storage of tools If tools are to give the best results, you must take care of them. Nothing ruins tools quicker than damp and rust, and sharp, cutting edges will soon become blunted and dented if left lying around. This means proper storage between jobs.

Some alternatives to the popular tool-box and the work-bench tool-rack are shown in Fig. 2. The first drawing shows a strongly-hinged tool-rack that will close and fit snugly behind a door. Useful if space is really short, and the tools are always handy. 2-4 illustrate a more elaborate idea for a tool-rack that can be carried about the house from job to job. With the support folded back (4) the frame can be stored away in a narrow space. 3-ply will be sufficiently strong for the board. Clips as shown and swivel pegs keep the tools in place.

The tool kit The choice of tools will depend on the type of work to be undertaken. If the main interest is in woodwork, a standard set of carpenter's tools will cover most work, although it may well be useful to add a fretsaw or fretsawing machine. Properly used, the tools shown in Figs. 3 and 4 will enable you to undertake a really wide range of carpentry jobs.

10

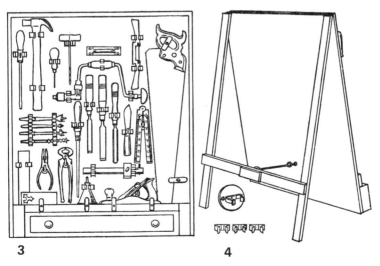

Figure 2. How to store tools in confined spaces and carry them easily about.

11

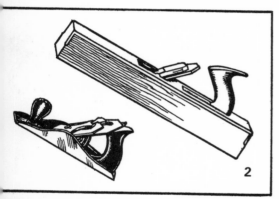

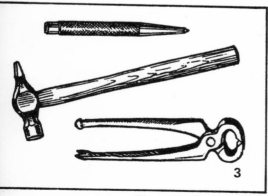

Figure 3. Basic tool kit.

For model making, a few specialized tools will be required unless you wish to work in metal. A razor blade, a really light hammer, a miniature screwdriver and a pair of small pliers will take one quite a long way.

Here, then, is the standard carpenter's tool kit.

1 Saws. Quite indispensable. A hand-saw somewhere between 18 in. and 24 in. will be sufficient for most general rough work and cutting thick timber. Good and poor saws don't look very different: make sure you buy a good make. A good blade should be absolutely flat and straight, and the teeth should show evenly on each side. A 12 in. tenon saw will be necessary for making joints.

2 Planes. Although the variety of planes on the market is really astonishing, the beginner will find a large Jack plane (about 14 in. long) and a smaller smoothing plane, for fine work and finishing, sufficient. Metal planes are more expensive than those made of wood, but they are much easier to use and set.

3 The hammer shown is a Warrington type and suitable for most jobs. Don't buy one that is too heavy, and don't let it be used for breaking coal. The nail punch is used for driving nails below the surface of the wood. The holes can then be filled with a

filler and ugly nail heads avoided. No matter how well you can drive a nail, you will need a pair of pincers more often than you think.

4 Chisels. The two shown here are firmer chisels measuring $\frac{1}{4}$ in. and $\frac{7}{8}$ in. across the blade. Firmer chisels will be used more than any other type, but a wider range of sizes, such as $\frac{1}{4}$ in., $\frac{3}{8}$ in., $\frac{5}{8}$ in., and 1 in., will be found extremely useful if funds permit. A wood-rasp and a triangular file will prove their worth for shaping.

5 A good drill and a wide range of bits is a must, together with a bradawl for boring small holes. A ratchet screwdriver with a properly insulated handle is the best type to buy, although not the cheapest. An electric drill is still something of a luxury, but it is one of the most adaptable and useful of tools. Apart from their usual role, they can, with suitable attachments, be used for sanding, grinding, buffing, sawing and wood turning.

6 For the handyman, pliers, spanner and glasscutter come under the heading of essentials.

In addition to these tools, you will need a vice. For woodwork the metal parallel-jawed vice is to be preferred to the older type of wooden vice. Undoubtedly the best type of vice for the model-maker is that which includes a ball swivel joint which allows

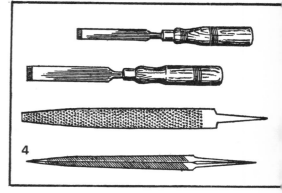

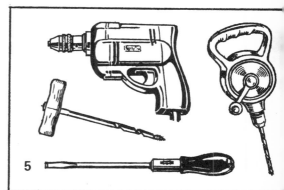

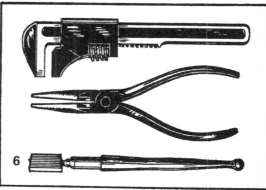

Figure 4. Basic tool kit.

it to be rotated to any position. They tend to be expensive, however.

Some types of parallel vice incorporate a clamp which is extremely useful in clamping together fairly wide sections of wood while glue or cement is setting. In any case, one or two C-clamps and corner clamps, together with a steel-bar cramp, the latter accommodating work up to, say, 1 ft. 6 in. in length, will be useful for carpentry work.

There are a number of other useful tools that may be added to your tool kit as they are required or when funds permit. A pad or keyhole saw will prove very handy for working in restricted places, and, of course, for cutting keyholes. A mortise chisel, a spokeshave—for finishing curved surfaces, a spirit level, and a wooden mallet will all find their uses for certain jobs, although it is possible to make a wide variety of things with the basic tool kit already described.

When planning your future tool kit, *always* remember the golden rule: *Always buy the best tools, they are cheapest in the long run.*

The only measuring instrument required to produce good results is a good stainless steel rule. The rule will also come in handy as a straight edge for testing work, and as a guide for scoring and scribing lines on wood with a marking knife. For the latter purpose, though, a marking gauge will make scoring very much easier.

It should be mentioned that when setting out measurements from a rule, readings should not be taken from the extreme edge of the rule since this tends to become damaged in time, thus causing inaccuracy. It is better to start from the first inch marking. Moreover, always mark off all dimensions from one given base line. If each dimension in succession is marked off from the previously marked line, errors are liable to accumulate and reach surprisingly large proportions if a fairly intricate piece of work is being marked out.

Handling tools Handling tools correctly is a skill that can only be acquired with experience. The only way to pick up the right knacks and tricks is to find someone who really understands tools and ask him to show you the basic points. Then practise yourself and when you go wrong, always ask again. In this way you will correct faults before they

Wood sculptures of stylised animals — a bull, penguin and hamster. The different grains and textures of the woods used give character to the mo—dels.

The complete range of Surform wood sculpture tools — Planer File, Standard Plane, Block Plane, Round File and Standard File.

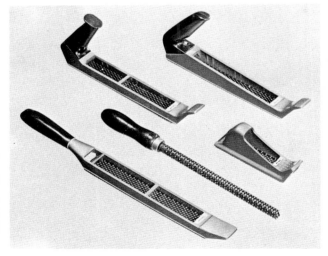

Stanley Works
(*Great Britain*) *Ltd.*

*Stanley Works
(Great Britain) Ltd.*

The graceful poise of the animal has been captured in this delicate sculpture in light-coloured wood.

Teachers World

This stool and bookcase were made by pupils of Adwick High School, Doncaster.

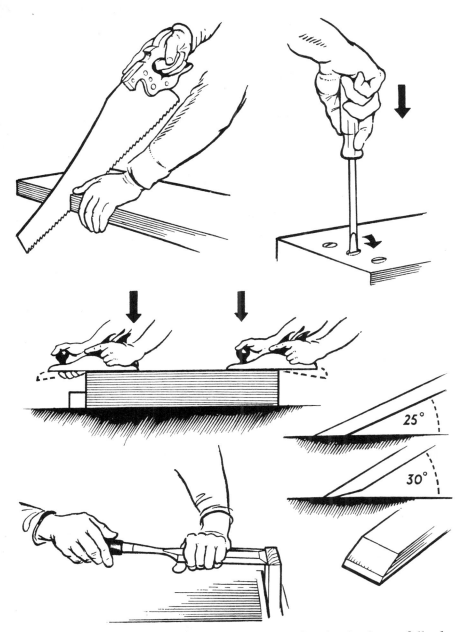

Figure 5. Tips on the handling and sharpening of tools. Study carefully the position of the hands. When sharpening a chisel, first sharpen blade at 25° on an oiled stone, then raise to about 30° to sharpen the cutting bevel.

15

become bad habits of working. And whenever you have the opportunity, watch a professional carpenter or craftsman at work.

Although it is impossible to learn how to use tools from a book, the drawing on the previous page illustrates a few preliminary facts on the handling of tools.

Sawing Hold firmly, but not tightly, with first finger along side of handle. Start sawing with up strokes, guiding blade with left thumb along the line to be cut. Stand looking straight down the blade. Do not work too quickly, use as much of the cutting length of the saw as possible and let the weight of the saw do the work (see Fig. 5).

Planing With a smoothing or jack plane (see Fig. 5), the handle at the back is used to push the plane whilst the forward knob is used to guide the plane's direction. *Always*, always plane with the grain, shave a little at a time, and check that you are removing wood evenly from the whole surface. Adjusting the blades of either a metal or a wooden plane will have to be learnt from experience.

Chisel work Paring across the end grain as shown in Fig. 5, press downwards, removing a little wood at a time. Chiselling with the grain should always be done with the left hand guiding the blade very firmly.

Nailing Both the work and the hammer must be firmly held otherwise damaged wood, or even fingers, may result.

Screwing Always remember first to drill a hole slightly smaller than the screw that is going to fill it, otherwise the wood is in danger of splitting.

Remember: 1 Learn to sharpen your chisels and plane blades as soon as you can. Blunt tools are next to useless. Rub metal tools over with an oily rag now and again.

2 Sharp tools can inflict a terrible injury in the hands of a young child. Make sure you store *all* your tools away as soon as you have finished with them.

3 If you take care of your tools, they will serve you well; if you don't, they won't; it is as simple as that.

Wood working and finishing

Carpentry opens up a wonderful world for the keen handy boy. However, before you can produce satisfying work, there are quite a few things to learn. Having dealt with tools and their handling in the last chapter, we can now pass on to the various types of joints, which being much more complicated, will be dealt with in detail, together with assembling and finishing. Before wasting your efforts and good timber, practise making them on off-cuts until you can produce good, neat, well-fitting joints.

Basic Joints   A tenon saw should be used for cutting joints. All the following joints and some of their many variations are shown on pages 18 and 19.

Half-Cut Through   One of the most useful and simple joints is the "half-cut through". It is generally used to make a flush joint between two pieces of wood by cutting away half the thickness of each member so that, when they are placed together, they make up the thickness of the original. But you must remember to take into consideration the thickness of the saw. Place the saw beside the marking line so that the slot cut by the saw will be entirely in the waste wood, and not added to the dimension of the joint, thus producing a sloppy fit.

Open Mortise   For connecting the ends of framing, the open mortise is a very handy joint. For this, as a rule, the tenon portion of the joint will be one-third of the total thickness of the two pieces of wood. Mark off first the exact position of the saw-cuts, both for the mortise and the tenon; the tenon itself can be completely cut with the tenon saw, the waste wood being sawn away after the tenon itself has been made by two cuts down from the end of the wood used. For the mortise two similar cuts must be made, and the waste wood *between* them taken out with chisel and mallet. For this work do not attempt to drive the chisel right

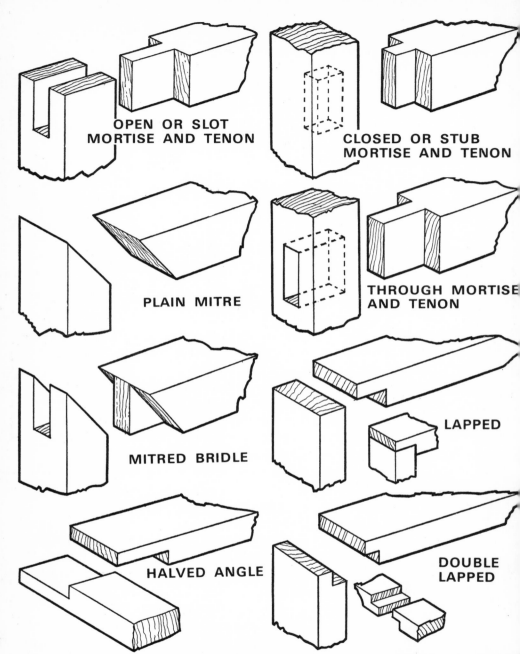

OPEN OR SLOT
MORTISE AND TENON

CLOSED OR STUB
MORTISE AND TENON

PLAIN MITRE

THROUGH MORTISE
AND TENON

MITRED BRIDLE

LAPPED

HALVED ANGLE

DOUBLE
LAPPED

18

Figure 1.   This illustration shows all the joints that you are likel
The rabbet and chamfer shown here are not, of course, joints,

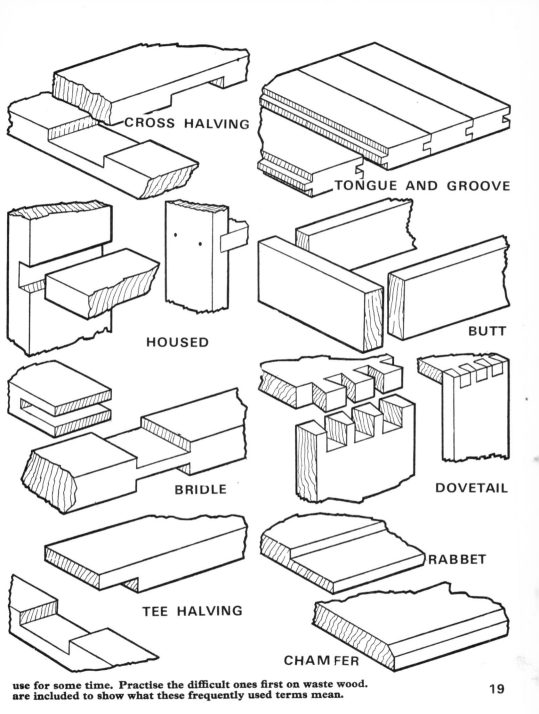

CROSS HALVING

TONGUE AND GROOVE

HOUSED

BUTT

BRIDLE

DOVETAIL

TEE HALVING

RABBET

CHAMFER

use for some time. Practise the difficult ones first on waste wood.
are included to show what these frequently used terms mean.

Figure 2. Here
are some of the
main types of
nails used in
carpentry.

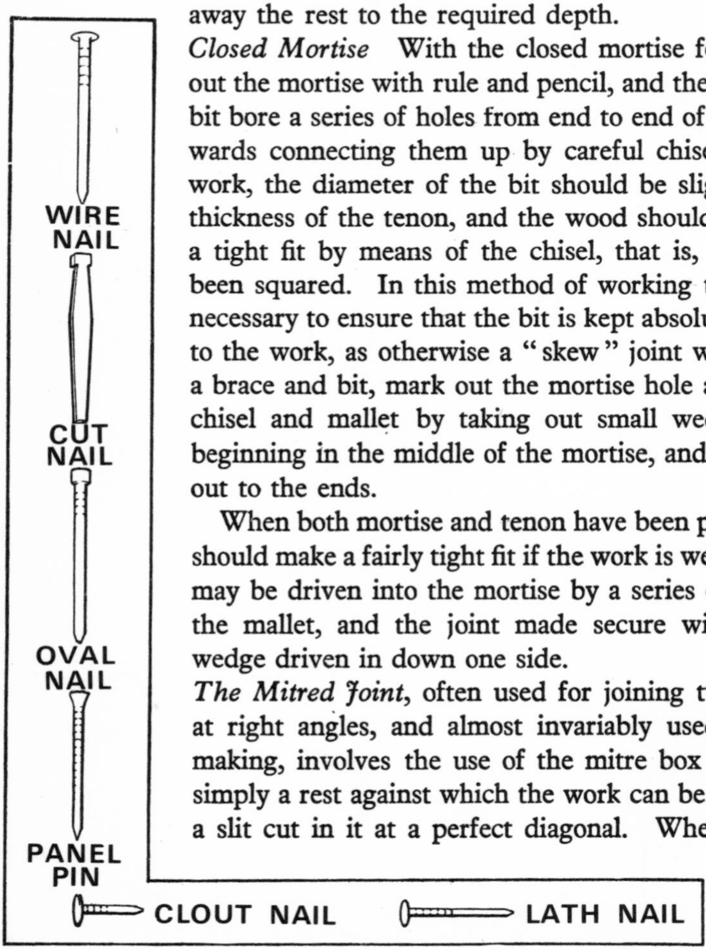

**WIRE
NAIL**

**CUT
NAIL**

**OVAL
NAIL**

**PANEL
PIN**

CLOUT NAIL   LATH NAIL

through the mortise, but tap it in for half an inch or less, and
then make a V-shaped cut toward the end of the mortise, in the
waste part of the wood, so as to remove a chip of half an inch
or less in thickness. Repeat this process until the chisel has
cut through the wood, and in doing it see that the chisel is kept
straight. It is safest, however, to cut out all but about an
eighth of an inch of the mortise, and then, with the chisel, pare
away the rest to the required depth.

Closed Mortise With the closed mortise form of joint, mark
out the mortise with rule and pencil, and then with a brace and
bit bore a series of holes from end to end of the mortise, afterwards connecting them up by careful chisel work. For this
work, the diameter of the bit should be slightly less than the
thickness of the tenon, and the wood should be pared away to
a tight fit by means of the chisel, that is, after the hole has
been squared. In this method of working the greatest care is
necessary to ensure that the bit is kept absolutely perpendicular
to the work, as otherwise a " skew " joint will result. Failing
a brace and bit, mark out the mortise hole and cut it out with
chisel and mallet by taking out small wedge-shaped pieces,
beginning in the middle of the mortise, and gradually working
out to the ends.

When both mortise and tenon have been prepared—and they
should make a fairly tight fit if the work is well done—the tenon
may be driven into the mortise by a series of gentle taps with
the mallet, and the joint made secure with a thin wooden
wedge driven in down one side.

The Mitred Joint, often used for joining two pieces of wood
at right angles, and almost invariably used in picture-frame
making, involves the use of the mitre box or block, which is
simply a rest against which the work can be fixed or held, with
a slit cut in it at a perfect diagonal. When the ends of two

20

pieces of wood have been cut by means of a tenon saw, they will make a perfect right angle when fitting together. This joint is perfectly sound so long as the finished work has some further support, as in the finished picture frame, when the backing and glass together hold the frame true; for open and unsupported framework, however, the mitred joint has not sufficient strength. Fastening of a mitred joint is best done by means of a screw set in the wood at right angles to the line of the join, and the wood should be countersunk so as fully to take the head of the screw and leave no projecting metal.

Dovetailing forms about the strongest and best method of making box joints. It is in reality a series of mortises and tenons cut in the edges of two pieces of wood, and requires considerable care. The slots should be marked off before any actual work is done, and it is most essential, in cutting the slots, to remember that the thickness of the tenon saw must go into the waste wood that will be chiselled out, not into the part that remains. But good dovetailing is difficult: practise first on some waste wood.

For ordinary box making, and for most rough work, one end of a board is simply placed against the end of another, and the two are nailed or screwed together. This in itself is a weak form of joint, but in box making the bottom of the box strengthens the end joints, and sufficient security is attained by this, the simplest of joints. It is about the only one that requires no practice.

Glues and Adhesives Secure joints must be glued. Glue is bought in flat cakes, which should be broken up with a hammer into small pieces, sufficient of which are placed in the glue pot to fill it a little less than half-way to the top. This is then just covered with water, the outer container is filled with water,

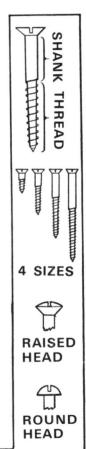

Figure 3. A selection of the main types of screws used in wood-working.

SHANK
THREAD

4 SIZES

RAISED
HEAD

ROUND
HEAD

CHEESE HEAD   COUNTERSUNK HEAD

and the double pot placed on the fire, gas or electric ring, and kept there until the glue becomes liquid. During the heating process the pot should be stirred to ensure that every bit of glue is properly dissolved; the resulting fluid should be only just thin enough to be worked on to the wood with the brush.

Frequent boiling causes glue to lose its strength, and therefore it is better to make a small quantity at a time if you are engaged on only a small job. A scum, which will be observed forming as the glue comes to full heat, must be removed or it will reduce the strength of the glue—and note, it must not be stirred in.

There are several kinds of glue made from animal hoofs, skins, and horns. That known as Scotch Glue is the strongest and best, and owing to the strength required in work for which glue is used, it is advisable to use only the best. If the glue is required to stand damp for any considerable period, there should be added to it a saturated solution of bichromate of potash, sufficient of this being added to turn the liquid glue to jelly while it is hot, and then just enough glue added to the mixture to restore it to a liquid state. Exposure to sunlight will render joints made with this glue perfectly water-resisting, and its strength is in no way lessened by the bichromate of potash solution, which any chemist will supply ready for use.

A number of liquid glues, plastic adhesives and cements have been placed on the market in recent years, and for special purposes these give good results if the maker's instructions are carefully followed.

Gluing As to the actual use of glue, it should be applied as hot as possible, and where practicable the wood or other substance that has to be joined should have its joining surfaces warmed before the glue is applied. In many cases, such as in most kinds of picture-framing, this can be done without any fear of warping the wood. Sufficient glue should be applied to cover the surfaces of the joint fairly thickly, and pressure should then be applied—by a press or clamp, if possible—to squeeze out practically all the glue, leaving the two pieces of wood as close together as possible. With small pieces of work, the two pieces to be glued together should be rubbed against each other after the glue has been applied, and before settling them into place for pressing or clamping, in order to drive out any air bubbles, and to work the glue into the tiny interstices of the wood. When a joint has been finished, the thinner the glue film between the two pieces of wood the stronger will the joint be, which is why as much pressure as possible should be applied to the work while the glue is setting.

After a joint has been made it should be given twenty-four hours to set under pressure. When the joint has set, any surplus glue that could not be wiped off at first should be carefully picked away with a chisel or knife.

In re-making an old joint, care must be taken to clean away every particle of old glue before applying fresh, or the joint will not set properly. New work, too, must be perfectly clean and free from grease of any description.

Finishing: Painting Nothing is more satisfying than to see your finished job painted, varnished or polished, and ready for use. Now, this final operation is often hurried or done in a slap-dash manner. Remember, painting is a skilled job, and if carried out properly will give your work a professional finish.

Four different brushes should be obtained; a "fitch", as painters call it, which is a brush with rather rounded hog-hair bristles; a flat hog-hair brush; a sash brush, which is a narrow and shaped brush for painting narrow slips, such as sash frames; and a brush with its edge cut on the slant. (See Fig. 4.)

Before painting make sure that the surface is dry and clean. New wood should be first rubbed down with glass-paper, and then given a thin coat of primer, which should be given a full day and night to dry. After this, all the inequalities of the surface should be filled in with a filler and sanded flush; generally there are indentations round the heads of nails, and other tiny holes of varying depth, which need to be closed up this way. When this has been done, the painting can be proceeded with, but remember the following points:

1 Three thin coats are far better than one thick one.
2 Let each coat dry thoroughly before applying the next.

3 Do not hurry by overloading your brush, dip only the point into the paint, brush surplus paint back into tin, and try just to wet the surface. Work with the paint.

4 Applying too much paint will cause unsightly running.

If enamel paint is used it is essential to put on an undercoat. This may be applied in a fairly heavy coat, and it should be allowed to dry quite hard, after which it may be rubbed down with glass-paper to get a smooth surface. Then the enamel itself should be applied in two

Figure 4. Useful kinds of paint

thin coats, each of which must be allowed to dry thoroughly, preferably in a warm room which is as dust free as possible. If the enamel has been carefully applied, and dust carrying draughts are excluded from the drying-room, the result will be a very fine, wear-resistant smooth surface.

In the actual application of the enamel to the work, the amateur may find difficulty in preventing brush strokes from showing. It is best to work the brush about as little as possible, especially for the last coat; the paint should be laid on with the brush, not worked in with it, and if the right quantity is applied, although brush marks may show faintly in working, the enamel will smooth down as it dries. Flat enamel, which gives a matt surface instead of a shiny one, is generally used on articles of furniture, and this is less likely to show brush marks than the glossy kind. The latter, however, gives a surface that is easier to keep clean.

When any job is finished, do not forget to clean the brushes thoroughly. After cleaning, the brushes should be washed out with warm water and soap, or detergent, and then thoroughly dried.

Finishing: Staining and Polishing Stains may be applied either with a brush or a sponge; they require considerably less care in their application than do paint or enamel.

24

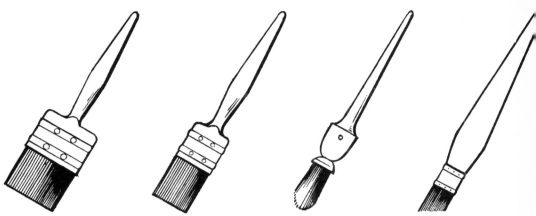
brushes. From the left: a distemper brush, two sizes of flat hog-hair brush, a rounded brush and a skew fitch.

If a glossy finish is required, let the stain dry in thoroughly, and then apply a coat of best carriage varnish with a flat camel-hair brush.

The most beautiful finish of all for woodwork is obtained by French polishing, which is no more than a matter of care and hard work. It is best to get the polish ready made up, and spirits of wine will be required for separate use in the work. The method of polishing is to dip a small piece of flannel in the polish, cover it over with a piece of fine, soft linen, and then rub the surface to be polished with a sweeping, circular movement, finishing off when the flannel is nearly dry by rubbing lightly with the grain of the wood. Then re-moisten the flannel, cover again with the linen, and repeat the process. For finishing, a separate rubber is slightly moistened with spirits of wine, and lightly applied with a circular rubbing movement of the arm. If this is not very carefully done, the effect will be to remove the polish already applied, and then the work will have to be done all over again.

Remember: work in small areas; it is the rubbing not the quantity of polish that produces a good result.

Making a simple bookcase and stool

These are the first of several carpentry jobs described in this section of the book. They range from the easy to the fairly difficult, and they may be looked upon as exercises in carpentry. For this reason, the instructions have been kept down to a minimum so that you may learn to use your own judgement. You will find it very good practice—particularly in the case of the dog kennel shown on page 34—to work out the construction details yourself.

Before attempting any carpentry job, however, the following fundamental rules should always be observed:

1 Check your plans carefully to determine the quantity of timber you will require and how economically it can be employed. Then check them again.

2 Mark up every single part of the job on your timber before even looking for the saw or plane. Then check it again—carefully.

In this way you will neither waste wood—and even the cheapest is expensive—nor will you order too much.

Timber Sizes Timber is sold by the foot, and those sizes which are most in demand are known as standard sizes, e.g. 1 in. by 1 in., 2 in. by 1 in., 3 in. by 1 in., etc., 2 in. by 2 in., 3 in. by 2 in., 4 in. by 2 in., and so on. Any size of timber other than a standard one, such as $2\frac{1}{4}$ in. by $1\frac{1}{4}$ in., will probably have to be cut and planed specially by the timber merchant, and will, therefore, be more expensive. When sizes such as this are required, it is usually cheaper to purchase the next standard size up and plane it down yourself. Most timber is sold "prepared, ready planed" and will be about $\frac{1}{8}$ in. smaller than the stated size on the depth and width. Remember to take this into account when calculating joints. Timber prices vary tremendously and it is only possible here to give a general idea of what each job will cost.

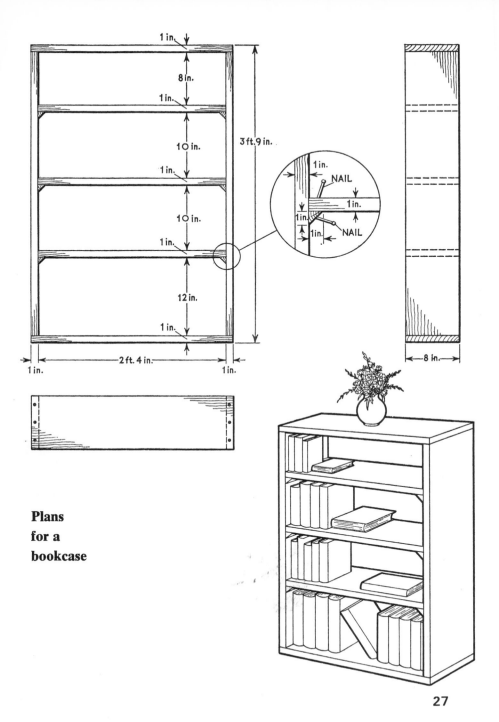

Plans for a bookcase

1: Making a Bookcase

Without proper shelving it is not long before books become dirty and damaged. And they are always in the way! The answer is to build a bookcase on the lines shown on the previous page. It is neat, strong, simple to make, and will hold a remarkably large number of books. The dimensions, of course, can be easily altered to suit a particular nook in a wall or any awkwardly shaped books you have. Look at your books first and see how they range in height.

   Timber required—ordinary white wood will be suitable:
   Frame and shelves—19 ft. 6 in. of 8 in. by 1 in.
   Cost—about 25s.

   The shelf supports can be made from wood and skew-nailed as shown, or metal angle brackets may be used and recessed for neatness. The sides, and top and bottom shelves should be screwed. Finish with either gloss paint or French polish. If the wood is attractively figured, simple waxing can give a very pleasant result.

2: Making a Small Stool

The stool opposite will find a useful place in almost any room in the house. Making it will provide excellent practice in producing good closed-mortise and tenon joints, and these tend to be tricky.

   Materials required: three different sizes of timber will be needed—$1\frac{1}{2}$ in. by $1\frac{1}{2}$ in., $1\frac{1}{2}$ in. by 1 in. and $1\frac{1}{4}$ in. by 1 in.

   For the last size you will probably have to buy $1\frac{1}{2}$ in. by 1 in. and plane it down. For the seat base you should be able to obtain a cheap off-cut of plywood, and foam rubber can be found at most surplus stores. Total cost—around £1.

   The seat covering may be made from almost any material you care to think of, although a strong furnishing fabric will stand the most wear. For a real touch of originality you could block print your own design on to some strong cotton. To ensure that the rubber fits on top of the base, make a paper pattern from the plywood and cut the rubber out from this. The frame can either be painted or French polished.

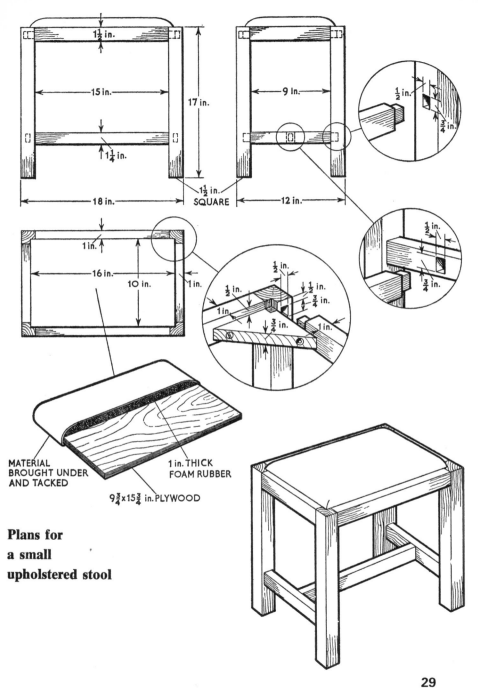

1½ in.

15 in.

17 in.

1¼ in.

18 in.

1½ in.
SQUARE

9 in.

12 in.

½ in.

¾ in.

1 in.

16 in.

10 in.

1 in.

½ in.

½ in.

½ in.

1 in.

½ in.

½ in.

½ in.

1 in.

¾ in.

¾ in.

¾ in.

1 in.

¾ in.

MATERIAL
BROUGHT UNDER
AND TACKED

1 in. THICK
FOAM RUBBER

9¾ x 15¾ in. PLYWOOD

**Plans for
a small
upholstered stool**

Making a clothes horse

Making a Clothes Horse

This simple carpentry job can produce a very useful result for wet Mondays. It is fairly easy to make, and if the work is carried out carefully, the finished clothes horse can look very attractive. Another point in its favour is that the only tools required are a hammer, saw, plane and chisel.

The joints needed are all through-mortise and tenons, and care is necessary if they are to fit well. If you haven't made a joint of this kind before, practise on some waste wood first. For additional strength the joints should be nailed as well as glued. Another method of securing them tightly is by driving two thin wooden wedges into the tenon, which will force it to expand. If the wedges are too large, however, the whole joint is in danger of splitting.

Timber required, which will cost about 12s., is as follows:

Sides—two sections—48 in. by $1\frac{1}{2}$ in. by 1 in.

Feet—two sections—9 in. by 12 in. by 2 in.

Cross rails—three sections—38 in. by $1\frac{1}{2}$ in. by 1 in.

The finishing of the wood is most important, for not only can a poor finish spoil the appearance of the work, but it can also damage clothes. A clear, splinter-free surface must be obtained, otherwise fine garments are likely to be snagged whilst being lifted off the rails. All the surfaces should, therefore, be sanded until perfectly smooth, and it is a good idea to round off the top edges of the cross rails, as well. The appearance may be further improved if the tops of the uprights are rounded off, too. The wood can be left quite plain, but as there is a danger of damp clothes becoming slightly stained from certain woods, a painted surface is the best finish. Staining the wood or waxing it should be avoided for the same reason.

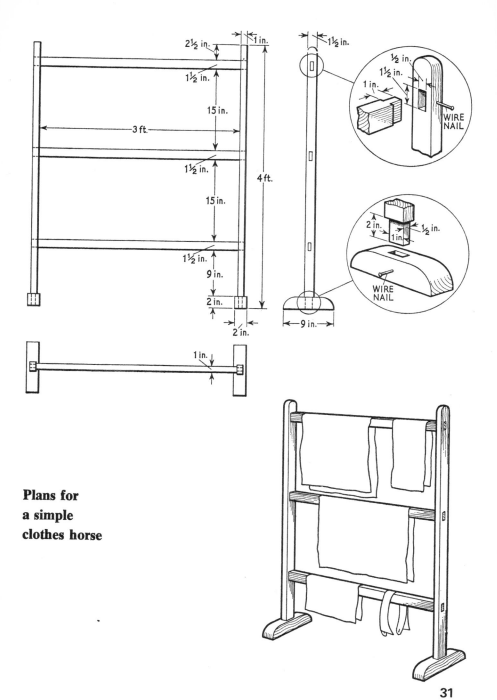

**Plans for
a simple
clothes horse**

Making a fire screen and dog kennel

4 5

4: Making a Decorated Fire Screen

During the warmer months of the year, the familiar, empty fire grate does not help to make a living room look its best, and a really attractive fire screen can be made quite easily to hide the gap. Basically, the screen shown here is no more than a frame standing on two feet supporting some kind of decoration mounted on the front of a piece of plywood backing. Many people, when making fire screens, tend to overload them with decoration and the result is frequently quite ugly. The most attractive results will be obtained if the frame is kept as simple as possible and the screen itself allowed to carry the full weight of whatever decoration you decide to use.

Unless one intends painting the frame, it is worth while—finances permitting—buying some attractively figured wood for a job such as this. The cost for the job will, of course, depend on the type of wood used. The quantities required are as follows:

Frame—84 in. of $1\frac{1}{4}$ in. by $\frac{3}{4}$ in. moulding.

Feet—two sections—6 in. by $2\frac{1}{2}$ in. by $1\frac{1}{2}$ in.

Backing—a single piece of $\frac{3}{16}$ in. three-ply 19 in. by 21 in.

The construction is not difficult. The sides of the frame should be mitred and then skew-nailed for strength, as shown. To ensure really tight-fitting joints, a mitre block should be used. The plywood backing is then screwed on. This makes the whole frame perfectly rigid. The making of the feet provides an excellent lesson in keeping a saw straight! But if you get into difficulties, finish making the angles with your small smoothing plane.

The decoration for the screen can be carried out in a very wide range of materials and designs, and before buying your timber it is a good idea to have an exact picture in your mind as to how you intend decorating the

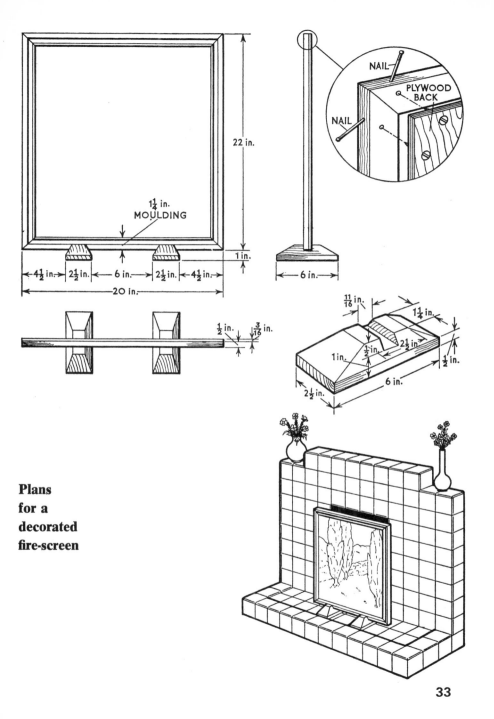

22 in.

1¼ in.
MOULDING

1 in.

4½ in. — 2½ in. — 6 in. — 2½ in. — 4½ in.

20 in.

NAIL

PLYWOOD
BACK

NAIL

6 in.

½ in.
3⁄16 in.

11⁄16 in.
1¼ in.
1 in.
½ in.
2½ in.
2½ in.
½ in.
6 in.

**Plans
for a
decorated
fire-screen**

33

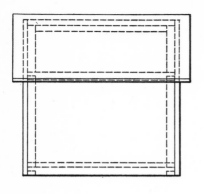

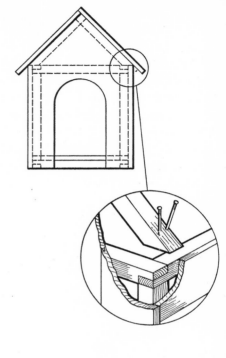

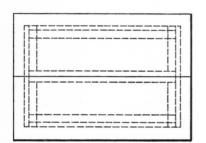

**Plans
for a
dog kennel**

screen. Then, if the frame is not going to be painted, a wood can be selected to harmonize or contrast with the screen.

The frame and feet can be finished as desired, of course, but although painting the wood can give very pleasing results, French polishing or plain waxing usually provides the most attractive finish. Avoid staining, it can easily make woodwork look cheap.

Certain materials, such as veneers, tapestry, a lovely piece of cloth or a panel of beautifully figured wood, can be used for the screen just as they are. Other materials will have to be made up in some kind of design. Ample scope for this kind of decoration is provided by marquetry, leather, coloured board or paper cut out into shapes, gessowork, barbolawork, and metals such as brass or pewter beaten into relief.

5: Making a Dog Kennel
Providing a dog is not made to sleep out of doors in cold weather, he may well enjoy sleeping in a kennel during the warmer months.

The size of the kennel will obviously depend on the size of your dog and this is why the dimensions have been omitted from the drawing. These you will have to work out for yourself. Now the question of size is very important, for the dog must have plenty of room. If he is cramped and cannot turn with comfort, the dog will quickly become miserable. On the other hand, if the kennel is too large, the dog may feel cold.

The best way to determine how much space the dog needs is to box him in on three sides with some boards or even pieces of furniture. Do this when he is lying stretched full length, and then when he is loosely curled up. This, *plus a sensible margin*, will give you your length and width. The roof must be tall enough for him to be able to stand comfortably.

The actual construction is relatively simple and consists of making a frame and boxing it in. The roof must be waterproof and is best made with tongued-and-grooved boards, which are then painted. If the boards are simply battened on, they should be covered with tarred material of some kind. The floor must be raised above the ground, otherwise it will become cold and damp. And remember to make sure there are no splinters on the inside of the kennel.

Odd jobs around the home

Even the smallest flat or house needs regular attention and maintaining if things are to run smoothly and not be the cause of constant irritation. Doors and windows stick, locks stiffen, lights fuse, window-panes get broken, taps drip, and a whole host of other things become worn and damaged in the course of time. Often the head of the household is just too busy with other matters to find the time to do all the necessary odd jobs, and frequently they are left until in the end an expert has be called in or a replacement bought—an expensive business.

This is where you can make yourself really useful and find that your efforts are well appreciated. The ways in which a handy boy can help around the home are many. Even without the use of the simplest tools, a trip about the place with nothing more complicated than an oil-can filled with a fine lubricating oil can be very useful and surprisingly interesting. So, find an oil-can, and see where a little lubrication can literally ease things.

Useful jobs with an oil-can If your house has iron-framed windows, more likely than not you will find that the hinges work stiffly, so that every time the window is opened or closed a strain is thrown on the frame which will eventually cause the glass to crack through the use of too much force.

This is a job calling for the use of a ladder, for the hinges cannot be reached easily from inside the house, so use one, and be sure that you wedge its feet so that it cannot slip whilst you are standing at the top, working. (Fig. 2.) This is very important.

You will probably find that the window-frames swing on a bolt, the top nut of which is provided with an oil-hole. Examine this nut and make certain that the oil-hole is not blocked. If it is, clean it out with an appropriately-sized drill or a nail of which the point has been filed spade-shaped, using either of these tools by twirling between thumb and finger.

Oiling can now be done, the window being slowly worked to and fro until it can be opened easily to its full extent. If, however, the stiffness does not disappear, it can be taken for granted that the hinge-bolt is really badly seized, and the nut should be unscrewed with a spanner or a pair of pliers, cleaned up with fine emery-paper, and oiled before replacing. This should settle the job.

Similar treatment can be given to the turning-pins of the window-

Figure 1. **Every room has use for the oil-can. Even in the dining-room the doors, windows, castors and drawer locks need occasional lubrication.**

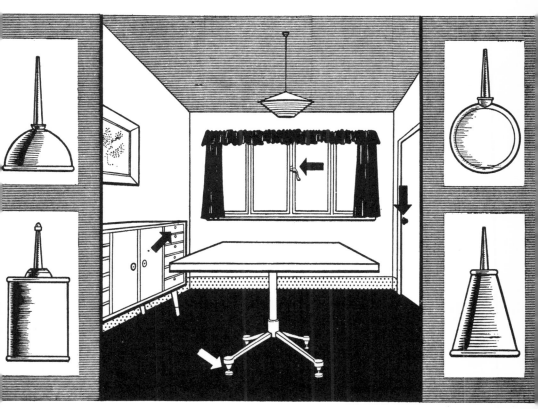

Figure 2. Never use a ladder, even if it is only a shortish one, without wedging the legs as shown here to prevent it slipping. Safety precautions such as this are often overlooked when doing odd jobs around the home, and can lead to serious accidents.

latch handles, but in this case great care should be taken during the unscrewing of the nut at the rear of the pin (between the bolt and the window-pane) to ensure that the glass is not cracked by clumsy use of the spanner. Once again it may well be found necessary to remove the pin completely and clean it, and when refitting, note that the pin has a flat side, which fits into the bracket on the window-frame and prevents the pin turning when the handle is used.

Oiling and maintaining locks Another place where the use of an oil-can is often very welcome is the inside of the 'mortise' locks used on the interior doors of a house, the simple mechanism of which is used every time a door is opened. No one ever seems to think of oiling a door-lock, even though each one in the house is used thousands of times every year.

Before oiling can be done it is necessary to remove the lock from the door, and Fig. 3, 1, shows how this is done. First, the grub-screw in one of the door-handles or knobs is removed and the operating rod withdrawn. Then the two small wood-screws in the edge of the door are unscrewed and the lock carefully prised out by inserting the screwdriver blade between the edge of the lock and the door-frame. Take care not to splinter the woodwork or chip the paint during this part of the job.

Now look at the flat sides of the lock. On one of them you will see a screw which is usually located centrally. Place the lock on a flat surface and remove the screw, after which the top half of the lock can be separated from the lower half to expose the mechanism, which should look something like Fig. 3, 2, which shows the return spring being removed.

38

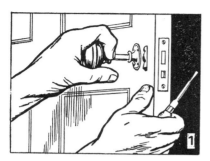

A little examination while the mechanism is moved with the handle will show where lubrication should take place. Do not use too much oil, but be sure that the oil you use is put just where it is required—at the rubbing and moving surfaces. (Fig. 3, 2.)

Incidentally, if this spring is found to be broken (as is the case in the drawing Fig. 3, 3, and does occasionally happen) it can be replaced for a few pence, whilst if the replacement spring is a trifle too long, it can be broken off to the correct length with the aid of the pliers as shown in Fig. 3, 4. Note carefully that the latch of the lock (which projects from the face of the box) must be in the "out" position before the spring is replaced.

Whilst on the subject of locks, a loose or badly-worn door-handle can be tightened quite easily. In some cases it is merely the handle grub-screw which is loose, but if tightening the grub-screw does not improve matters, a washer can be cut from cardboard, felt, or linoleum, which should be placed between the door-frame and the handle (see Fig. 4); the latter being pressed firmly into place before inserting the grub-screw and tightening it. If this does not work, new handles are probably needed.

Figure 3. How to oil a mortise lock and replace a broken spring.

Lubricating a cylinder lock

Figure 4. Stopping a handle from rattling with a cardboard washer.

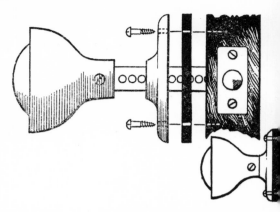

Lubricating cylinder locks
The Yale and similar cylinder locks that are used on millions of front doors should never be oiled, but lubricated with graphite. If oil is used to lubricate a cylinder lock, the oil will eventually form a sticky sludge with the dust that seeps into the lock and the delicate mechanism will tend to seize up.

Get an old "BB" pencil, cut off an inch or two with a table-knife, and extract and finely crush the lead; then mix with it a little vaseline to make a graphite paste. A little of this should be applied with a pointed matchstick to the key-hole of the lock and the key worked in and out to distribute the lubricant among the "tumblers" inside the cylinder (see Fig. 5). On no account use too much paste, nor use paste that is too thin, otherwise the lubricant will surely find its way into trouser-pockets and handbags; and your work will not be appreciated!

Oil in the bathroom Another thing in the house which never seems to get its fair share of lubrication is the moving arm of the lavatory-pull, where it passes into the cistern. How often it is that the operation of this simple piece of machinery is so hard and noisy that one feels almost

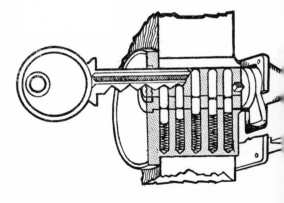

Figure 5. Cylinder locks should be lubricated only with graphite.

40

certain that one is going to pull the cistern from its moorings every time it is used!

In this case, the use of oil is useless because of the water in the cistern, so vaseline is used—or some of the graphite-grease already made for the front-door lock. The method is as follows: lift off the cistern cover if there is one, and immediately behind the shaft of the pull-crank will be found a split-pin which prevents the shaft from being pulled out of its bearing. Bend the ears of this pin straight and pull it out of its hole. The pull-lever can now be withdrawn from the cistern sufficiently to allow grease to be smeared on the shaft—which should be done quite liberally. Then return the shaft and replace the split-pin.

Keeping the castors rolling   At first glance you would not imagine that there was anything which wanted oiling in the lounge—except, perhaps, the clock; but this is not the case, and never attempt to oil a clock or watch movement. (This is a job for the watchmaker.) More often than not you will find that the easy chairs and the settee are very difficult to move about, and, nine times out of ten, this is due to the castors not having been oiled since the furniture was bought.

Up-end one of the chairs and examine its castors. Do they revolve freely and swing round without binding? If they do not, the discreet use of the oil-can will work miracles, but you had better advertise the fact; otherwise the next time someone draws a chair up to the fire they will get the surprise of their life! But don't use too much oil, or the carpet will suffer.

And so, you see, that by just wandering around the house with an oil-can, you can find many simple little jobs crying out to be done which you can easily do with no more complicated tools than a screwdriver and a pair of pliers.

Simple repairs
to the plumbing

Plumbing is the trade which deals with the fixing and repairs of the various pipe-work about a house: the sink and bath drains, the water-supply, and—many years ago—the gas supply. It is a complicated trade which takes years to learn and there is not a great deal which the handy boy can do about the house with regard to the plumbing, but in the winter there is sometimes an " S.O.S." when a water-pipe gets frozen and bursts, and it is then that you can take charge and make an emergency repair which may have the effect of saving many pounds' worth of damage to ceilings and household goods. But—and this is important—you must know exactly what to do and how to do it.

Burst pipes Let us suppose that the water supply pipe to the lavatory cistern has burst, as shown in Fig. 1, 1. Water will be dripping or squirting out in an alarming manner and something has to be done—and done quickly, otherwise before you know what's happening the floor will be inundated and the water will be through the ceiling into the room below —with disastrous results.

First. Turn the water off at the main. If you have not already found the main tap (or stop-cock, as it is termed), search in the front garden or front path to the gate until you find the small round or square metal plate covering the hole in which the stop-cock is buried. A screwdriver or pointed poker will usually serve to lift the lid, and at the bottom of the hole disclosed you will see the tap, which must be turned in a clock-wise direction until it will turn no further. If you find it impossible to turn it (it may not have been turned for years and is often very stiff) get a short length of 2 in. by 1 in. wood and saw-cut a V-shaped nick in one end to act as a key to place over the handle of the tap.

Don't think that your time is wasted when making this tap-key, for no

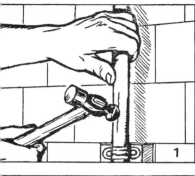

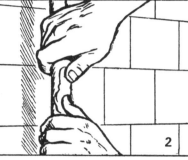

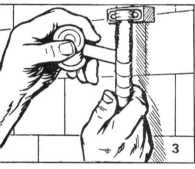

pipe repair is possible until the main stop-cock has been turned off. (It is, however, a sensible idea to try this main tap during the summer and thereby save hectic and time-wasting minutes should a burst occur. Then, if it is stiff, make your key and be prepared.) It is possible, however, to *reduce* the flow of water from the burst pipe by hammering the sides of the crack together as shown in Fig. 1, 1.

In some houses a second stop tap is fitted to the main inlet pipe inside the house. Providing the burst has not occurred before this tap, it can be used to check or completely stop the water supply to the rest of the system.

Having turned the water off, the part of the burst pipe around the crack should be wiped absolutely dry and a pad of well-softened putty applied to cover the crack generously (Fig. 1, 2), after which insulating-tape or elastoplast can be wrapped round pipe and putty as shown in Fig. 1, 3. This will produce a very effective temporary repair. The water can then be turned on again and the house supply restored whilst waiting for the professional pumber.

To cope with a really serious burst, when for some reason the mains supply cannot be stopped, the fractured pipe may be cut on the supply side of the burst and hammered over (Fig. 1, 4). Alternatively, the pipe may just be hammered flat instead of being cut. This will also check the flow of water to the burst. But in each of these cases, the work facing the plumber when he arrives is considerably greater, and therefore more expensive, than that caused by the putty-and-tape method.

Figure 1. Emergency repairs on burst pipes. 1, Hammer the crack together; 2, Cover crack with putty; 3, Bind tightly with insulating tape; 4, With a very severe burst the pipe can be cut and hammered flat.

Insulating pipes But prevention is better than cure; and the handy boy can save himself a lot of work by getting up in the loft and taking a look at the piping to see whether it is properly protected in the event of a severe frost (see Fig. 2). If it is not, several thicknesses of old newspapers can be cut into 6 in.-wide strips and wound round the pipes and tied into place with string. Lengths of old blanket may also be used to insulate the pipes from the freezing temperature often experienced in lofts in cold weather. Fig. 2 shows other methods.

Thawing frozen pipes However, assuming that such precautions have not been taken, and it is discovered, when the thaw takes place, that water is not flowing—say—to the bathroom or the hot-water supply cistern; then obviously the appropriate supply pipe must be blocked solid with ice. This entails special treatment.

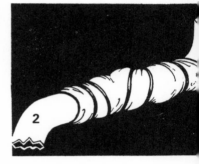

First, trace the pipe from the cistern to which water is not flowing and locate it in the loft. Then wrap a piece of old blanket or other absorbent material round it and, placing a piece of mackintosh or a bowl under the offending pipe, pour boiling water over the pipe, moving along until the whole of the pipe has been treated. (Fig. 3, 1.) When the frozen part is reached, you will hear the water break through the thawing ice inside the pipe and the noise of the cistern filling. The job is then completed.

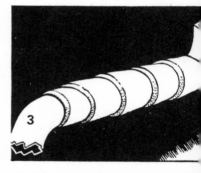

Another way is to get a bucketful of almost boiling

Figure 2. Unless properly insulated pipes may freeze and burst in cold weather. The insulating methods shown here are: 1, 'Fibreglass' stripping; 2, Rags or sacking; 3, Felt; 4, Corrugated paper.

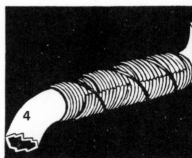

44

water and swab the pipe from end to end with a flannel dipped in the water, continually renewing the flannel with hot water until a break-through takes place (Fig. 3, 2). Wear the thickest rubber gloves you can find! In very obstinate cases, a blow lamp may have to be used as shown in Fig. 3, 3. But this treatment is rather risky, for if the pipe is heated too rapidly it is likely to burst. For this reason it is a method best left to experts.

Never use an electric fire to thaw a pipe as Fig. 3, 4. If there is an earth-leak on the fire and you happen to touch a water-pipe and the fire at the same time you may receive a very severe shock indeed.

Tap repairs Household water-taps wear out in time and leak. If there is one which continually drips, even though it is turned "off", it is the

Figure 3. **The right and wrong ways of thawing pipes, described in the text.**

internal washer which needs replacement. If, however, water exudes from the point where the shaft of the tap enters the body, it is the packing-gland which needs replacement.

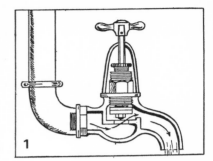

For the repair of a dripping tap, the water must first be turned off at the main and the pipe leading to the tap drained of water by turning on the tap. A spanner is then placed on the hexagonal nut (which is underneath the cover of modern taps, but is exposed on those of older types) and this is undone by turning in a *clockwise* direction (that is, in the opposite direction to that usually used for undoing nuts). Fig. 4, 1-5. When the handle and stem of the tap has been thus unscrewed, there will be found a rubber, fibre or leather washer mounted in a brass holder inserted in a hole in the lower end of the stem. The washer is screwed to the holder with a brass screw, which must be undone before the washer is removed and replaced with one of exactly the same diameter. Before replacing the whole unit, take care to see that the handle of the tap is fully in the "turned-on" position before screwing the unit tightly down, otherwise the new washer will be ruined immediately.

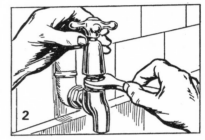

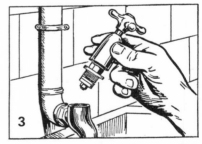

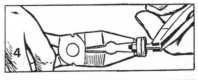

Treatment of a tap from which water seeps at the stem-gland consists of undo-

Figure 4. How to renew a worn tap-washer.

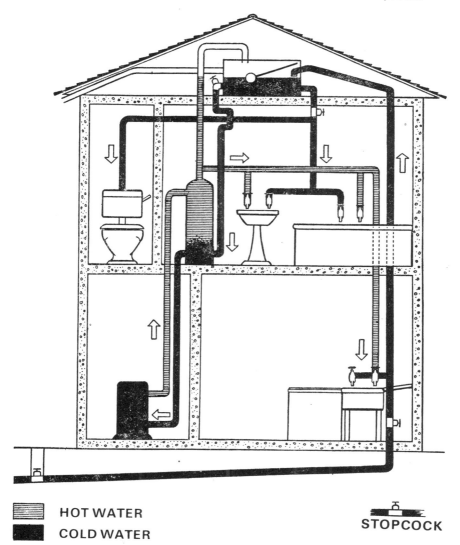

HOT WATER

COLD WATER

STOPCOCK

Figure 5. Very few houses have identical water systems, but the layout shown here illustrates the basic principles for a small house. The system in your home may well have variations; discover what they are and find where the vital stop-cocks are situated.

ing the gland-nut (Fig. 6, 1), pulling out the worn-out packing, and replacing it with loosely-stranded string or sisal-cord which has previously been soaked in lard. Do not screw the gland-nut down on the new packing more tightly than is necessary to stop the leak.

Sometimes a tap becomes loose or twisted where it is screwed into the water-pipe, and in this case, all that is needed is to unscrew it for a few turns, wrap round the exposed thread a few turns of fine string or coarse cotton soaked in paint, and re-screw until the tap is in its correct position—upright (Fig. 6, 2).

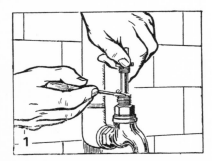 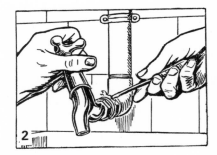

Figure 6. Stopping a leaking tap by packing it with greased string.

Blocked sinks and basins Still in the kitchen, there is another job which crops up now and again—the waste-pipe from the sink gets blocked. The same trouble can occur in the bathroom wash-basin. This is rather a messy job, unless the pipe can be un-blocked without opening the plug at the bottom of the trap below the sink or basin. Always try the following methods of clearing the pipe before opening the trap-plug.

If you do not possess a force cup (Fig. 7, 1), fill the sink with water and, taking an old basin, place it under the surface of the water, inverting it over the waste-pipe hole. (See Fig. 7, 2.) Now suddenly lift the basin and press it down again suddenly over the hole several times. The pressure of water thus produced in the pipe will usually clear it, and, if successful, the sink should be emptied and swilled down with *boiling* water, which will remove the accumulated cooking fat in the pipe which was probably the cause of the blockage.

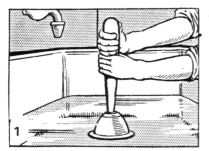

If the pipe is stopped-up by sediment it will be necessary to unscrew the plug at the bottom of the trap, and the handle of a spanner can be used to do this; but, before removing the plug, a bucket must be placed below to catch the muck and water. (Fig. 7, 3 and 4.) The sink should then be well flushed with hot water, which is allowed to drain into the bucket. Do not over-tighten the plug when replacing it and do not put any unnecessary strain on the trap-pipe when unscrewing or screwing-up the plug.

Air locks Occasionally an air lock will form in a pipe and either cause severe noise and vibration, or block the flow of water altogether. The best method of curing this trouble is to fit a length of plastic or rubber tubing from a tap that is working freely to the tap on the pipe that is impeded. Then turn the free-running tap full-on and slowly open the other tap. The pressure of water should force the air in the pipe back into the tank, leaving the water to run freely. If this method fails, turn off the stop-cock controlling the part of the system affected and drain all the water from the pipes.

Figure 7. Every kitchen sink gets stopped up from time to time. Here is how to unblock it.

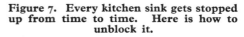

Ten trouble-saving tips

1   Always use nails rather than wood-screws for fixing into the end grain of wood.

2   If nails tend to split wood, cut off the points and drill pilot holes of a slightly smaller diameter than the nails being used.

3   Never forget to allow for the width of the saw-cut when cutting wood to size.

4   Always keep the face of your hammer brightly polished.

5   Always thoroughly wet adjacent surfaces when using plaster.

6   An enlarged hole in a wall or in wood can be successfully plugged with match-sticks dipped in adhesive and cut off level with the face of the work.

7   A tear in a carpet can be joined by smearing a strip of cloth with rubber solution or some other quick-setting adhesive. This makes a good substitute for sewing.

8   To stop outside paintwork, which receives plenty of sun, from blistering, give the wood a coat of oil-bound distemper before painting.

9   Always grease wood-screws before inserting them. It will make them easier to remove if required.

10   To tighten a loose hammer-head, knock the end of the handle, not the head, on the ground. If the handle is still loose, drive a thin wedge of wood into the opening at the head end of the hammer.

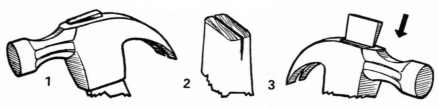

Simple electrical maintenance

" Safety First " should be an absolute rule when carrying out these little electrical jobs which are suggested as being well within the scope of your capabilities. Remember, one cannot be too careful when dealing with the house electricity supply, and if you are in the slightest difficulty, or feel that the job you have been asked to do is beyond you, never hesitate to call in an electrician. A handy boy—or a handy man, for that matter— is never an expert, and a professional man will often save far more than his services will cost. Do not, therefore, attempt to do more than the four electrical repairs mentioned below—at least without further advice, and if needs be, assistance from a senior member of the family.

ALWAYS, ALWAYS SWITCH OFF THE HOUSE SUPPLY BEFORE DOING ANY ELECTRICAL REPAIRS. And this means switching off *every* main-switch in " the cupboard under the stairs " or wherever the company's main wires enter the house. Then try every light and heating socket in the house to be certain that everything is absolutely " dead ". It is then safe to proceed—NOT BEFORE.

Mending fuses If one or more of the lamps in the house fails to light, the cause may well be that the lamp has burned out, so, before going to the trouble of checking the main fuses, a new lamp of correct voltage and wattage should be tried in the lamp-holder. (The voltage and wattage of a lamp are stated clearly on its brass contact-clip or on the bulb itself.) If a new lamp does not effect a cure, proceed to the fuse-box or fuse-boxes alongside the meter and, first switching off the main-switch applying to the fuse-box under inspection, pull out each china fuse in turn and check to see that the fuse-wire between the brass screws is intact. (Fig. 1, 1.) Always remember that a fuse may *appear* to be perfect, yet not be contacting each screw. The test for this is to try to pull the fuse-wire out of

51

Simple electrical jobs

Figure 1. Electrical jobs you can safely tackle.
1. Mending a broken fuse. Remember that before you touch any metal part of the fuse, the *main current* must be switched off and the fuse removed from the box.

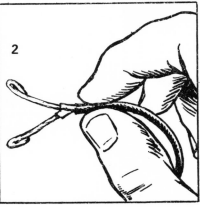

2. When fitting a new lead to a plug or switch it is a good tip to double the ends of the wire over. This ensures a good contact.

3. How to fit a new flex to a ceiling rose and correctly support the weight of the lamp and shade.

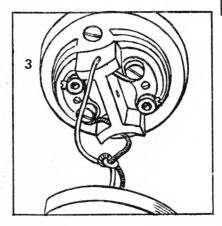

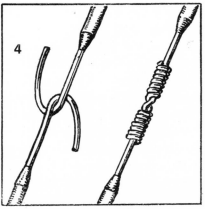

4. The correct way to splice two wires together to make sure that there is a proper contact between them.

the hole through the china block with a pin or small screwdriver. If it has blown inside the hole, you will be able to fish out the end, in which case the wire must be replaced with *exactly similar* wire of the same material and thickness. "Any old piece of wire" *will not do.* Many disastrous fires have been caused by the use of the wrong kind of wire for electric fuses on the house supply. Incidentally, the fuse-wire should be wrapped round the screws in a clockwise direction, so that, as they are tightened, the wire remains in position; but the screws should not be done up so tightly as to snap the wire. Also, if it is seen that the "blown" fuse consisted of two strands of wire, it is important that the two strands replaced are twisted tightly together before being placed under the screws.

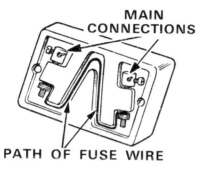

MAIN CONNECTIONS

PATH OF FUSE WIRE

Figure 2. Another type of fuse to that shown in Figure 1, 1. The principle of repairing it is the same.

Always cut off any stray or frayed ends of fuse-wire before replacing the fuse-block in the box.

Wiring work When fitting a plug or other connection to a piece of household electrical equipment, the wire end must be properly bared so that the copper wire is placed in direct contact with the plug ends. To do this the outside sheathing of the two wires comprising the flex should first be carefully pushed back to expose the pair of insulated wires within. Then each of these in turn should have its rubber or plastic covering carefully removed *without cutting or damaging the wire inside.* (This is very important.) The ends of the bare wire (about $\frac{1}{2}$ in. in length) are then folded back as shown in Fig. 1, 2, and poked through the holes in the plug or lamp-holder before doing up the retaining screws therein.

Similar wire-baring tactics are used when a new piece of flex is being fitted from a hanging lamp-holder to a ceiling-rose (Fig. 1, 3), where it will be seen that a knot is tied in the wire a few inches back from the end which will allow the weight of the lamp and shade to be taken by the rose-cover instead of by the screws holding the wire. The same clockwise method of passing the wire ends round the screws as that already mentioned is used here.

Where wires have to be joined, their ends are first bared, then temporarily hooked together, before being twisted as depicted in Fig. 1, 4. In the case of flex wire, the individual strands of flex in each wire must first be twisted together, then each wire is "married" by twisting as shown. After this, each wire-joint is wrapped with insulating-tape for

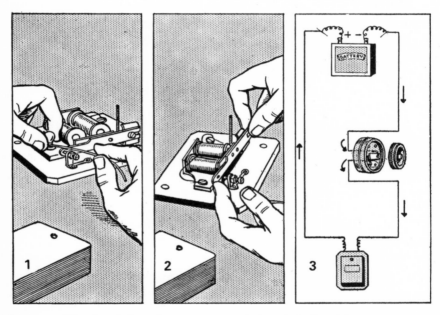

Figure 3. The circuit for a battery-operated electric bell and how to test it for faults in the terminals and bell.

half-an-inch on either side of the actual joint; and, finally, the pair of insulated joints are treated to an overall wrapping of insulating tape, which will make a joint which is electrically as well as mechanically strong.

When fitting a lead to a plug for use in a power point, it is important to remember that the three separate wires in the lead must be connected to the right part of the plug, otherwise you may blow the fuse. With electrical appliances run on power, the plastic sheathing of the three wires in the lead are of different colours: the brown wire carries the positive charge, the blue wire carries the negative charge, and the green / yellow wire is for the earth. Inside the plug, the three pins terminate in connections that are marked P (positive), N (negative), and E (earth). Sometimes there will be a colour identification to correspond with the colours used for the wires, as well, but all you have to do is to ensure that the brown is connected at P, the blue wire at N, and the green / yellow wire at E.

And this is about all that the handy boy can safely do by way of repairs and additions to the house electric supply, but once again, do remember to SWITCH OFF AT THE MAINS FIRST! Shocks are very dangerous things.

Repairing an electric bell But there are other electrical jobs you can do about the house without having any reason to worry about safety precautions, and the front-door electric bell which refuses to ring presents just such a job well within the capacity of the handy boy.

In Fig. 3, 3, is shown the electrical circuit of a door-bell. It will be seen that the current flows from the battery — (negative), through the bell-push (when it is depressed), through the bell (or buzzer), and so back to the battery—+ (positive). It is therefore quite easy to understand that, if there is one break in this circuit, the bell will not ring when the button is depressed. Neither will it ring, of course, if the battery is " flat " or exhausted!

If a new battery does not cure the trouble, check the bell or buzzer by touching a flash-lamp bulb across its terminals when the bell-push is depressed. If the lamp lights, the fault is in the bell. (Fig. 3, 1.) Remove the cover of the bell and see that the end of the screw which presses against the sprung strip which carries the hammer is clean and bright— also the little button of metal on the sprung strip itself. If they are not clean and do not come into contact when the bell is at rest, use some fine emery-paper to clean them up and then bend the fixed end of the sprung strip carefully so that the screw-point *just* touches the button. (Fig. 3, 2.) Then try to bell-push again, and if without success, the fault must lie in the push itself, the contact points of which must be cleaned after the cover has been removed. (Fig. 3, 3.)

Repairing window frames and window panes

From time to time windows have the annoying habit of sticking. There are two main causes for this and they can both be remedied without much difficulty.

Frequently, the sticking is due to one or more of the hinges becoming loose, which results in the window dropping slightly out of true with the surrounding frame. Tightening the screws again will quickly correct this although sometimes the screw-holes will have become worn through friction, in which case a few slivers of wood, or even matchsticks, will give the screws sufficient new wood to bite on. Occasionally, if the hinges have been loose for some time, the hinges may have worn shallow depressions in the window or the frame and it will be necessary to remove the hinges and build up the wood beneath to its original height with pieces of wood or hard-board.

The other main cause of window jamming arises from new coats of paint being painted on top of the old, until, in time, the thickness of the accumulated paint is sufficient to jam the window. To counter this, sand down one side of the window with wet-and-dry sandpaper—used wet—until the window closes without hindrance. Remember to take into account the new coat of paint that you will apply to match up with the rest of the paintwork!

Repairing a sash-cord window Sash-framed windows should be periodically examined to see that the sashes (the moving portions) work freely; otherwise serious damage can occur should the sash-cord break because it is rotten.

If you look closely at the window you will see that the sashes slide up and down in channels which are formed by wooden beads which prevent the sash from slipping outwards and from fouling each other. (Fig. 1, 1.)

56

At the bottom of these channels, on each side of the window-frame will be found the covers to the counterbalance-weight compartments, which, when removed, give access to the cords and weights.

From the weights the sash-cords run up inside the pockets, over pulleys fixed at the top of the window, and then downwards again where they are attached to the sides of their respective sashes on both sides of the movable frame.

Figure 1. Removing a sash-cord window is not a difficult job providing
Continued over

Assuming one of the cords is broken, the repair is commenced by first removing the parting bead, which is not a fixture, but can be prised out with a screwdriver, the blade of which is inserted beneath the bead at a short distance from the bottom. Take care not to split the beading. (Fig. 1, 1.) Next remove the inner guard bead in the same way, working from its centre and partly withdrawing the nails until it can be sprung out of the corner mitres. (Fig. 1, 2.) The sash can now be withdrawn by pulling it forwards and sideways. It can be rested on the window-ledge.

Now remove the cord from the frame by withdrawing the nails and open up the sash-weight pocket by removing the cover with the screwdriver. Then remove the weight and cut the broken end of cord from it. (Fig. 1, 3.) The next job is to oil the pulleys, after which the new cord must be fed through over the pulley until its end appears at the

the steps illustrated here and described in the text are followed closely.

sash-weight pocket. (Use only the very best cord. Even the strongest cord will wear out in time, however, and it is a better idea to fit light chain instead—but once again only the best quality should be employed.) If any difficulty is experienced in getting the cord or chain to pass down the weight-box, a heavy weight of some kind should be fixed to the end of a piece of string and dropped down over the pulley. When the string appears at the lower end of the pocket, it may be tied to the new cord,

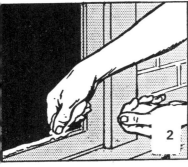

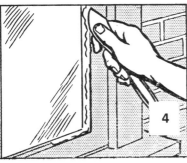

which can then easily be pulled through. (Fig. 1, 5.)

Now pass the end of the cord or chain through the hole in the weight and fasten it so that the fastening will not foul the sides of the weight-pocket, when the sash is operated. Pull the weight up until about 2 in. from the top of its run, (Fig. 1, 4), and wedge the pulley so that the weight is prevented from falling. Then replace the window-frame into its groove on the opposite side to that being repaired, and stretch the cord or chain down the side of the frame until its end is level with the bottom of the groove cut in the side of the frame, then nail it in place with half-a-dozen clout nails. Now try the sash in its proper position to see that it works correctly—and that the cord is of the right length. If it works freely, replace the parting beads, guard-beads, and pocket-covers, and the job is completed. (Fig. 1, 6.)

Replacing a broken window-pane To replace a broken window-pane, first break out *all* the old glass with a hammer, and do it gently. Then take out the hard putty with a strong knife, hammering on the back of it if necessary. (Fig. 2, 1.) When this has been done, it is advisable to give the recess the pane fits into a coat of quick-drying paint—any colour will do. This will prevent the wood sucking all the oil from the putty.

Now measure up the window-frame, and give the glass-merchant the measurements—less $\frac{1}{8}$ in. in each direction to allow for any slight variation

Figure 2. The main steps in replacing a broken window-pane.

in the window-frame and the expansion of the glass in warm weather. Purchase some putty—a lump about the size of your fist will be enough for an average-sized window-pane—and work this up in your hands until it is soft and pliable; then press it firmly into the recess in the window-frame (Fig. 2, 2) in readiness to receive the new pane.

Now press the glass carefully into position—firmly but gently—and when it is seated at about $\frac{1}{8}$ in. from the inside of the frame, drive in a few small glazing-pins to keep it in place if the window-frame is a wooden one. (Fig. 2, 3.)

More putty is then pressed into the groove and smoothed down with a moistened knife to give an even finish. (Fig. 2, 4.) Note: always use an old pair of gloves when handling glass to save yourself from being cut.

MORE HINTS AND TIPS

1 When screwing two pieces of wood together always be sure that the hole in the piece nearest the screw-head is large enough to take the un-threaded shank of the screw, and that the hole in the other piece is slightly smaller. This will enable the screw to draw the two pieces together without splitting the upper piece of wood. Do not use unnecessary force when driving wood-screws.

2 A good adhesive for sticking fabrics can be made by mixing together $\frac{1}{2}$ lb. of flour and 2 oz. of powdered rosin and slowly bringing the mixture to the boil with sufficient water to make a thick paste.

3 Partly-used tins of paint or enamel should be stored upside-down so that, when they are required for use, the skin which forms on the surface of the paint remains at the bottom when the tin is placed the right way up.

4 When a small screw has to be fitted in an awkward position, it is a good idea to get a match-stick, sharpen one end down to a chisel point, and press it into the saw-cut in the screw-head. In this way the screw can be put in place and given a few turns to start the thread.

Repairing upholstery

Another interesting home job is the repair of a sagging easy chair or one of which the seat has become lumpy because its springs have become displaced or are broken. Indeed, in ninety-nine cases out of a hundred, the failure causing the sagging can be rectified with a few yards of new webbing, a hammer, and some tin-tacks.

Renovating an upholstered chair In Fig. 1, 1, is shown the internal layout of a spring-seated chair. It will be seen that the spiral springs are arranged vertically under the seat, and that they are held by string stitches to strong material which goes right under the cushion of the seat, whilst at their lower ends they rest on, and are stitched to, a lattice-work of tightly stretching webbing. As we have observed, when the seat sags and becomes uncomfortable, the usual reason is that this bottom lattice of webbing has given way, or has become badly stretched; thus allowing the springs to fall over sideways. All that is then necessary is the fitting of new webbing and the re-stitching of the springs in position.

Re-webbing To re-web an average easy chair completely, about 10 yards of 2 in. wide webbing should be obtained, together with a gross or so of large-headed tacks about $\frac{3}{4}$ in. long. Needed also is a piece of wood about 2 in. by $\frac{3}{4}$ in. in section and about 6 in. long.

Take the new webbing, fold the end double, and tack the double thickness down to the framework of the chair—the framework of which should, of course, have been previously cleared of all the old tacks and frayed ends of webbing. (Fig. 1, 2.) Do not cut anything from the full length of webbing, as all the strips are attached working from the length.

Carry the webbing from the secured end to the other side of the frame, when it should be folded over the 6 in. piece of wood. Grip both the wood and the webbing in one hand as shown in Fig. 1, 3. It will be seen that the end of the wood is in contact with the side of the chair-rail and is tilted up a little. The block thus forms a lever, and, when it is depressed, the webbing is stretched tightly. Without releasing the downward pressure on the block, tack the webbing in place, then cut it about 2 in. behind

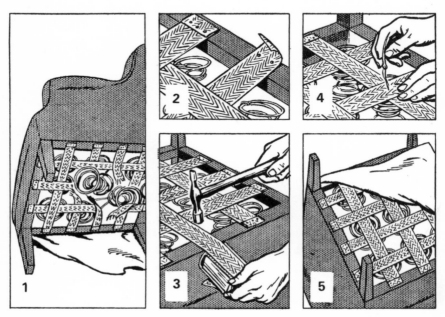

Figure 1. An old upholstered chair can often be made comfortable again by re-webbing, and sewing the springs back into place.

the tacking-point, fold it over, and drive more tacks through the double thickness—taking care to miss the tacks underneath.

Follow up by putting the first strip of webbing at right-angles to the first, and continue, first in one direction, then in the other; *weaving* the strips over and under each other as shown in Fig. 1, 5, and getting as nearly the same tension as possible on all the strips.

Sewing the springs Now we come to the sewing of the springs to the webbing, and this is done with a large straight needle and strong twine or thread. A professional upholsterer will probably use a strong curved needle, and if you can get hold of one of these you will find that it makes the job very much easier.

Use a long length of twine at each threading, and, placing each spring centrally at the intersection of the webbing, sew from underneath up close

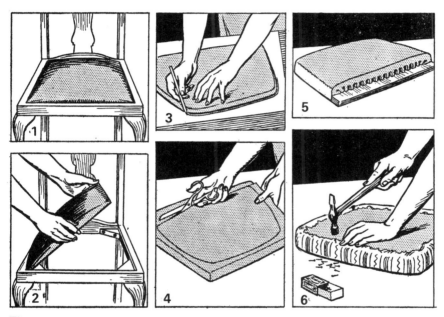

Figure 2. How to upholster a chair seat in foam rubber.

to the lower wire of the spring and down again exactly opposite and at the same time closely to the wire. (Fig. 1, 4.) Tie a single knot after the first stitch, then take three more stitches at points around the spring and back again to the first stitch. Do not cut the twine, but take a few stitches through the webbing toward the next spring, planning to have the last stitch alongside it. Make sure that each spring in turn is really securely attached. Then re-cover the bottom.

63

Foam rubber upholstery An entirely new method of re-upholstering old furniture has been made possible in recent years by the development of foam rubber, which is an ideal cushioning substance that can be used for seating and eliminates the need for the use of padding and springs. Before attempting anything ambitious with foam rubber it is recommended that you re-upholster a smaller piece of furniture such as a small occasional chair.

Foam rubber is available under many trade names in 1 in., 2 in. and 3 in. thicknesses and will be cut by the dealer to the approximate length and width required, to be later shaped from a home-made pattern to suit the chair. The procedure for re-upholstering a chair is as follows:

First, remove the old seat from the chair (Fig. 2, 2), then strip off all the old upholstery, taking care not to damage the woodwork, so that the seat can be measured accurately for its new cushioning. (Fig. 2, 3.) The old seat cushion can then be used as a pattern to mark out a paper pattern for the new cushion, but when cutting out the paper pattern an extra $\frac{1}{4}$ in. all round should be allowed for pulling-in the upholstery.

Now stick the paper pattern lightly on to the foam rubber and cut around the line with a pair of scissors. (Fig. 2, 4.) Next stick the foam rubber to the base of the old seat with a few dabs of special cement, but, before covering the seat, make sure that the foam rubber conforms to the shape of the seat. (Fig. 2, 5.) Then cut out the desired covering material to the shape and size required, again allowing extra for turn-over—in this case at least one inch all round. The seat cover is then carefully stretched and tacked all round to the underside of the seat-bed (Fig. 2, 6), and the seat replaced in the chair.

It will be seen that the old plywood or other base of the seat is used in this method, so that manipulation of woodwork does not enter into the job.

An alternative to the seat being supported by a wooden base or springs and cloth webbing, is the resilient rubber webbing that is now manufactured by an Italian rubber company and readily available in this country. This material is made from reinforced rubber strip and is simply nailed into position, being woven over and under in the same way as cloth

Design Furnishing
Contracts Ltd.

Coffee table and stool made from beechwood on clean straightforward lines. The stool has a detachable cushion with a zipped loose cover.

Nailing webbing across the seat of a chair—the material used here is a very strong rubber.

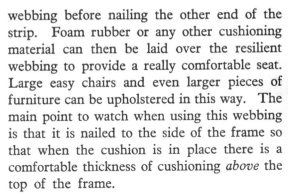

START

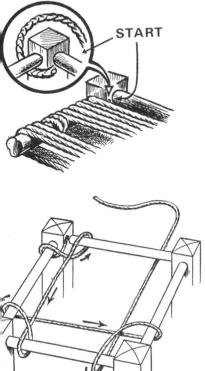

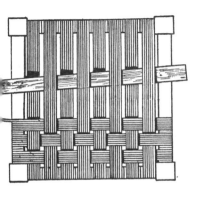

webbing before nailing the other end of the strip. Foam rubber or any other cushioning material can then be laid over the resilient webbing to provide a really comfortable seat. Large easy chairs and even larger pieces of furniture can be upholstered in this way. The main point to watch when using this webbing is that it is nailed to the side of the frame so that when the cushion is in place there is a comfortable thickness of cushioning *above* the top of the frame.

Making a cord stool-seat Another repair which broadly comes under the heading of upholstery is that of re-weaving the cord seat of a stool such as that shown in Fig. 3. The job is a very simple one, and, providing you start right, a very nice new top can be made for a few pence.

Purchase a good quantity of whatever " cord " it is desired to use—twine, raffia, or coloured twine—and tacking one end as shown in Fig. 3, 1, form a starting " square " of cord as depicted in Fig. 3, 2. Weaving is then continued, as shown in Fig. 3, 3, using a sharpened lath to raise alternate layers of weaving so that the cord can be passed easily through and the pattern produced. Of course, if desired, various coloured cords may be used with good effect, the various lengths of coloured cord being knotted together on the underside, where the join will not be seen.

Figure 3. New seats can be made for chairs and stools in a variety of materials. Shown here is the technique of reseating a stool with twine, cord or strong raffia.

65

Furniture
repairs

The joints of furniture which have been placed too near the fire will become weakened due to the glue on the joints drying out and shrinking. To avoid having to make major repairs it is important not to put off the tightening of loose joints and the repair of broken legs and chair rails for longer than can be helped.

Repairing loose joints Where there has been no excessive shrinkage, first remove all traces of the old glue by carefully knocking the leg assembly to pieces (Fig. 1, 1), and washing with vinegar. Next rinse the legs and rails in warm water and allow them to dry.

Although there are a number of excellent ready-mixed glues and adhesives on the market, Scotch glue will still be found to give the best all-round results in furniture work, providing it is properly used.

A thin coating should be placed on each of the surfaces to be mated and time given for it to soak into the wood before the application of a second thin coat. The second coat should be allowed to become tacky before fitting the two parts together, after which a mallet should be used to drive the legs into the seat. (Fig. 1, 4.) Care must be taken to ensure that all the joints between the rails are properly in place before this final hammering is carried out, and each leg should receive a blow in turn, so that no excessive strain is placed on any of the joints during the process.

When all is in place, two or three turns of stout string must immediately be wound around the four legs (Fig. 1, 5), tying it as tightly as possible and adding additional tension by inserting a stick of wood and twisting, as shown. Twenty-four hours should be given before this cramping is removed.

Mending broken chair legs In the case of a broken leg or rail, this is

66

treated as shown in Fig. 1, 1 and 3, being glued, panel-pinned and finally retained in place by twisting round with string; the latter being removed after the glue has set and the rail cleaned up with warm water, which will remove any excess glue. Fig. 1, 2 shows the old centre-pin being removed from a side-rail before re-assembly, a new panel-pin being driven in and the hole plugged with wood-filler or a mixture of glue

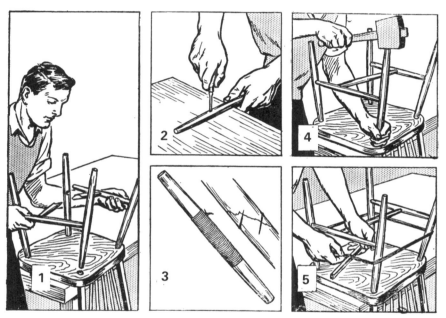

Figure 1. How to mend a chair with a broken rail and loose joints.

and sawdust, which can be tinted to match the rest of the woodwork.

Blistered and loose veneers Where dampness or heat has caused veneer on furniture to become loose, it should be repaired immediately to prevent further damage; blistered veneer should also be treated before the blister cracks open. Both these jobs are well within your capabilities, and here is the way to do them.

Where the veneer is loose, first remove as much of the old glue as possible from between the veneer and the base-wood by using vinegar and a thin, sharp knife. Try to do this without loosening any more of the veneer. Then, using the same knife, spread a thin coat of glue as far back as possible under the loosened veneer, and leave the glue until tacky. Then press the veneer gently back into place; afterwards wiping off any excess glue with a cloth dipped in warm water. Next, lay a sheet of thick cardboard over the repair, and, covering this with a piece of half-inch-thick wood, tightly clamp down and leave for at least two days.

The method of treating a blister is first to bathe it and the surrounding surface with hot water and then carefully cut around one side of the raised part to turn the blister virtually into a flap, which can then be treated as already explained. (Fig. 2, 1-4.)

Replacing damaged veneers Should the veneer also be damaged, it will be necessary to replace completely the offending piece. To do this, a piece of veneer as similar in appearance as possible to the existing surface should be placed over the damaged part, and both layers cut through with a very sharp knife or a single-edged safety-razor

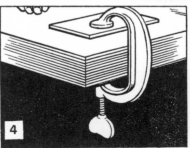

Figure 2. A badly blistered veneer is very unsightly, but it can easily be repaired as shown here.

blade. (A pen-knife is not the most suitable tool.) The zig-zag cut shown in Fig. 3, 1 is the best to use, as it gives additional strength to the repair and helps to prevent the new piece of veneer being broken off.

The damaged veneer is then very carefully pared back to the line of the cut (Fig. 3, 2) and any old glue removed from the base-wood. Then coat both the wood and the new piece of veneer with a very thin coating of glue. When tacky, lay the new veneer into its appointed place. It must be pressed down as hard as possible—even pressing with a hammer through thick cardboard—whilst the glue is setting. (Fig. 3, 3.) This is followed by clamping down, as already explained, after which any excess overhanging the sides can be cut away as shown in Fig. 3, 4.

Fitting a new castor When fitting a new castor to a chair or settee you may well find that the old screw has broken off short in the leg with its end below the surface, Fig. 4, 1. Now this is a common trouble and to get round it you will need a special tool which can easily be made from a 6 in. length of $\frac{5}{8}$ in. gas-barrel, which can be purchased at the ironmonger's. Place the length of pipe

Figure 3. Showing the main steps in repairing a veneer that has splintered along the edge.

in the vice and, with a triangular file, file a series of nicks in its end; thus turning it into a cutter for use in a hand-brace. (Fig. 4, 2.)

Place the cutter-tube over the broken-off screw in the leg and you will rapidly be able to bore a hole, leaving a centre-core in which the screw is embedded, and which can then easily be broken away and extracted. Next a piece of round wooden rod (dowel-rod—you may have to carve this yourself) is glued into the hole thus made. (Fig. 4, 3.) The new

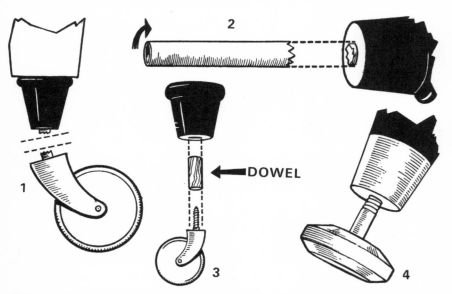

Figure 4. How to replace a castor that has broken off at the shank.

castor is fitted by drilling a new hole—after the glue has thoroughly set, of course.

There are, of course, alternatives to the castor shown in Fig. 4, 1. The castor (Fig. 4, 4), looks very attractive on modern furniture, and another type, shaped like a ball, enables pieces of furniture to be moved with great ease and speed.

Repairing broken table-legs The golden rule for all furniture repairs is to do them as soon as possible after the breakage has taken place, for when this is done the broken edges are clean and sharp and the parts will re-fit together so perfectly that the repair will be hardly noticeable. Take the case of the repair of one of the tapered legs of a kitchen table, for this job is not difficult.

If the break runs diagonally across the leg, as shown in Fig. 5, 1, all that has to be done is to apply glue thinly to the broken surfaces, match them perfectly, and hammer them into place; putting the table upside-down for the purpose. The glued joint is then tied round with string and allowed to set hard, after which screws or nails can be added to give additional strength. (Fig. 5, 2.) If driven well into the wood the heads can be covered with a wood filler and sanded flush. Alternatively, wooden dowels can be fitted, for which holes are bored after the glue has set. (Fig. 5, 3-5.)

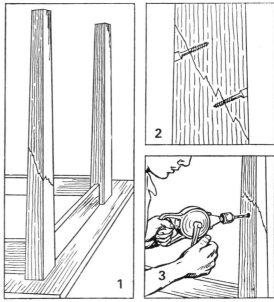

Figure 5. Repairing a cracked or broken table leg without replacing the entire leg

Round table-legs can be repaired as described above provided that the break runs diagonally across the leg, so that a good gluing surface is available. If the break is directly across the leg, it is a matter for dowelling. But this operation requires great accuracy and skill if the finished job is to be presentable.

Sticking doors or casements Although not strictly a furniture repair, it sometimes happens that doors and casements drop and hang at an angle instead of perpendicularly, causing sticking. Usually this is due to the top hinge working loose. In this case the screws should be removed from the top hinge and slightly larger ones substituted, or else the holes should be tightly plugged with wood and the old screws re-inserted. In some cases, however, although the hinges both seem tightly screwed, they

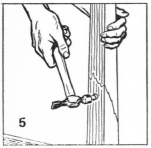

(continued from page 71)

have, in fact, dropped slightly, either where fixed to the door or casement, or where fixed to the jamb. If the drop is only slight, it is best to pare away with a sharp chisel a very slight thickness from the bottom of the door or casement, to prevent sticking.

Loose drawer knobs Drawer knobs which have become loose in their holes can be fixed quickly and permanently by plugging the hole with one or more match-sticks which have been previously dipped in glue or adhesive and cut off flush with the front of the drawer. The shank of the knob should also be smeared with adhesive.

Sticking drawers Sticking drawers can easily be repaired, and, where the trouble is only slight, it sometimes can be cured by rubbing the drawer runners with candle-wax dripped from a burning candle. In cases where the bare wood has become swollen by dampness, however, a cure can usually be effected by partially opening the drawer and setting an electric light bulb inside to dry out the wood thoroughly. But in the case of wear of the runners, the only thing to be done is to replace them with strips of hard wood.

To do this, the lower edges of the sides of the drawer must first be carefully sawn off, as shown in Fig. 6, 1, and new strips of correct size glued and tacked in place to provide new rubbing surfaces. Care must be taken to punch the heads of the securing panel-pins well down below the surface of the strips so that they do not score and damage the lower runners. This is done with a nail-punch or the end of a really large nail, and, of course, a hammer.

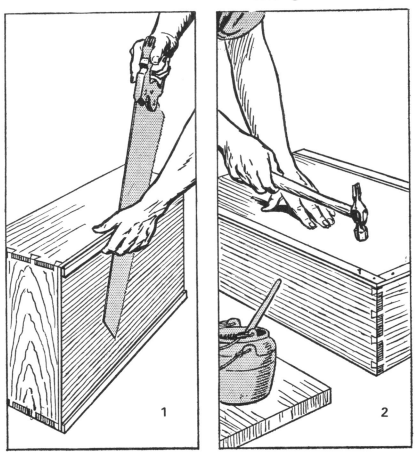

Figure 6. Renewing the worn runner on a badly sticking drawer.

Replacing drawer stops Drawers are also apt to become worn with constant use, so that they can be pulled right out when fully opened. This very common fault can be cured by the fitting of a new "stop-strip" at the rear edge of the bottom of the drawer, as shown in Fig. 6, 2, in which case adhesive and panel-pins should be used for fixing.

A check should also be made to see that the stop-blocks on the front

73

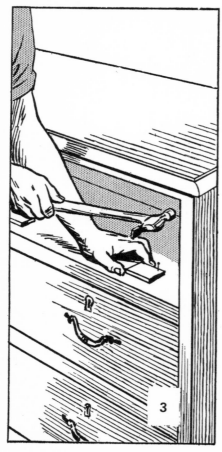

Replacing the drawer stops.

edge of the drawer-frame are not unduly worn. If they are they should be replaced by new ones as illustrated in Fig. 6, 3, but care should be taken that the new blocks are not much thicker than those they replace otherwise difficulty will be experienced in returning the drawer to its place. This later part of the job is, incidentally, done by placing the drawer in its runner whilst the front of the drawer is depressed, then gradually raising it.

Other repairs One of the most skilled repairs you can attempt is to replace the wood surrounding the keyholes in a really old chest of drawers which have become badly worn over the passing years. The method of doing this is to remove the locks and chisel either a diamond or rectangle of wood from around the keyhole. If the finished job is to have a really professional appearance, the diamonds or rectangles must be small, exactly the same size and in the same position. A small, very sharp chisel is needed. When you have perfect, clean holes, the new pieces of matching or contrasting wood must be cut. These pieces must *fit exactly* and it is the most skilful part of the job. When you are sure that the pieces will fit without any movement in the hole, the keyholes should be cut. This is done by drilling a small pilot hole and then opening them up with a keyhole saw. Then all is ready for gluing.

Useful jobs
and essential tips

Hanging pictures

To hang a picture frame so that it has the right amount of forward tilt from the wall, the eyelets or lugs should be inserted at a distance from the top of the frame of one-quarter of the frame's total length. The cord or wire is then tied to form a triangle with its top point or apex coming at one-third of the distance from the eyelets to the frame's top. (See Fig. 1.)

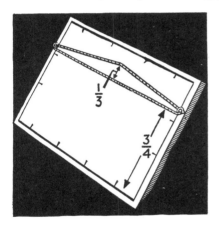

Figure 1. How to hang a picture.

Painting over creosote

It is not possible to paint over creosote without brown stains showing through the coat applied. This may be avoided by first painting with aluminium paint, but it is important that the creosote is thoroughly dry before this is done.

Laying Linoleum

Before you lay a new piece of linoleum always make sure that there are no tackheads projecting above the floor-boards which will damage the linoleum after it is laid. Such tacks must be removed, not hammered down into the floor. Always use a sharp knife for cutting linoleum and, as it spreads after it has been in place a few months, always cut it slightly undersize—allowing about $\frac{1}{4}$ in. in every three yards.

Repair to Lavatory Cistern

If the lavatory cistern continues to fill up and overflow it is usually due to

Figure 2. Temporary repair to a cistern.

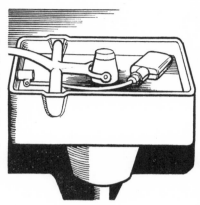

the ball-float leaking and refusing to float. A good temporary repair can be effected by tying a corked bottle to the ball-float arm after the punctured float has been removed (see Fig. 2). The punctured ball can be replaced, of course, but if the ball is made of copper and the puncture small, it is interesting to heat the ball to remove any water inside and try to solder over the hole.

Drilling a hole in glass

An easy way to drill a hole in glass is to make a little ring of putty around the place where it is desired to make the hole and pour turpentine into the recess thus made (see Fig. 3). Drill the hole slowly with an ordinary twist-drill, but do not use too much pressure. When the tip of the drill appears on the underside of the glass, turn the sheet over and repeat the process on the other side. A little emery powder sprinkled around the tip of the drill will speed the process, but the drill will need re-sharpening before being used again for normal work. Special glass-cutting drills with tungsten tips can be bought, however.

Curing slipping mats

Mats which have an irritating way of slipping can be easily cured by sticking strips of thin rubber (cut from an old cycle inner-tube) at each end (see Fig. 4). Rubber solution should be used as an adhesive. Alternatively, the whole mat can be backed with a sheet of thin rubber.

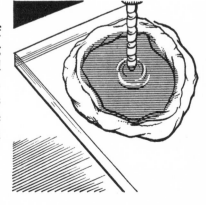

Figure 3. How to drill a hole in glass.

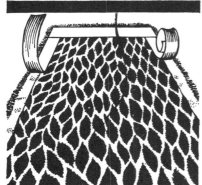

Figure 4. Stopping a mat from slipping.

Care of paint brushes

If properly cared for, good paint brushes will last for years—but they must be looked after. Immediately you have finished painting, clean your brushes—they should never be stored away with even a trace of paint on them. This is especially so if emulsion paint has been used, for this type of paint dries extremely rapidly and is insoluble when dry, easily ruining the brush.

Brushes used for oil-bound paints are best cleaned first in turps substitute, paraffin, or any white spirit. Then fill a jam jar with warmish water and plenty of detergent, and stub the brush up and down until it is thoroughly clean. After this rinse the brush in cold water, shake all the moisture from it, smooth the bristles and store away. Providing it is not tight, an elastic band can be slipped over the bristles to keep them in place. If you have to stop painting for say an hour or two, your brushes can be left in water as shown in Fig. 5, instead of being completely cleaned. This will stop the paint on the bristles from hardening.

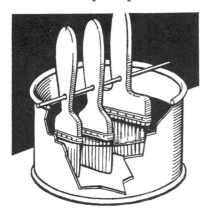

Brushes used for emulsion and distempers should be washed in *cold* water the *moment* you put them down. Wash until every sign of paint has disappeared. Then dry and store away.

Never leave any brush standing for days or weeks in water or spirit.

Never store brushes resting on their bristles. They are best stored flat, or hanging by the handles. (See Fig. 6.)

Figure 5. A useful tip for cleaning brushes.

Tips for looking after your tools

1 Never use a tool for any other purpose than that for which it is designed. (Never use a screwdriver as a lever or a chisel as a screwdriver, for example.)

2 Never put files in a drawer in such a way that they rasp one against the other.

3 Always keep metal twist-drills in a tightly-fitting tin box in which a little oil has been poured. It will stop them rusting.

4 Never use a heavier hammer than is necessary for the job in hand.

5 Never use a metal-headed hammer with a wood-chisel, and never use a hammer with a screwdriver for any job. (The proper tool to use is a metal chisel.)

6 Never use unnecessary force when tightening a screw or nut. The smaller the screw or nut, the less amount of strength required to tighten it properly. Undue force will only strip the thread.

7 Always remember that until you know exactly how to sharpen your tools, it will pay you to get them sharpened professionally. Good woodwork cannot be done with blunt tools.

Figure 6. Storing brushes correctly.

8 After using a saw cutting trees or shrubs in the garden, remove any sawdust clinging to the blade and, if you are not going to use the saw for some days, wipe the blade over with an oily rag.

Painting and decorating

These days, the redecoration of a room is by no means the difficult task that it used to be before the invention of the paint roller, with which simple, yet ingenious tool it is possible for a beginner to make a tip-top job of painting walls—either with oil or water-soluble paints.

As with all jobs, however, there is a right and a wrong way of working, so let us see how to redecorate your bedroom by painting over the existing wall-paper which has become faded and torn and has come away from the wall in places. In other words, how to give the room a refresher treatment which will not cost much and yet which will completely alter its character.

A word about paint First, what kind of paint should be used for this type of job? There are literally hundreds of different makes of paint on the market, but what concerns us here are the basic types, which are listed below. As with all other materials, use the best quality you can afford. Cheap paint often looks fine to start with but it never wears as well as a good paint; it chips and cracks, and you will find that cheap paint covers nothing like the area that the same quantity of a better quality paint will.

Paints for ceilings and walls

Emulsion paint: This paint has a plastic base. It is very popular and widely used today. It has many advantages and it can be easily and successfully washed when it gets dirty. Emulsion is ideal for walls, gives a lovely finish and is easy to apply. Allow 2 hours between coats.

Distemper: real distemper is oil-bound. It is very good but it has lost some of its popularity since the introduction of emulsion paint. Allow 4 hours between coats.

Ceiling white: an oil-bound distemper specially prepared for use on ceilings.

Colour washes: these are cheap paints of poor quality and are sometimes mistakenly called distempers. They are, however, made from powdered colours and water and do not give very lasting results. Their only advantage over emulsion paint and distemper is their cheapness.

Paints for woodwork

Oil-bound paint: probably the best all-round paint for woodwork. They will give excellent, smooth, durable finishes. They must always be used with an undercoat. Allow 24 hours between coats.

Synthetic paints: these paints give satisfactory results for woodwork but they show a tendency to chip. Allow 24 hours between coats.

Varnish paints are cheap and give fair results, but they cannot be compared with oil-bound paint. Allow 4 hours between coats.

Lacquer paints give a very high finish but they cannot be used for large areas of wood, such as doors. They are useful for painting small articles, bathroom cabinets, towel rails and the like.

The drying times quoted for the above types of paint will vary with the particular make and the weather conditions at the time of painting.

Now, to get down to it.

Preparing the woodwork First, of course, all the furniture must be moved into the middle of the room to provide a clear working space at the walls, and the whole lot must be covered with old sheets—or a dust-sheet.

Next remove the lock-plate, handles, and finger-plate from the door and draw any odd hooks, nails or screws from all the woodwork, afterwards filling the holes with a cellulose filler and levelling off. Similarly, if there are any cracks between the skirting-board and the wall, these, together with any actual holes in the latter, must be filled with a cellulose filler before the painting begins.

Now rub all the paintwork down with No. 00 glass-paper or wet-and-dry sandpaper, used wet, working in a circular manner where you can.

The next thing is to wash the paintwork carefully. Sugar-soap may be used for this but most decorators these days use a preparation called

*tanley Works
(Great Britain) Ltd.

Making a table :
a) the completed base

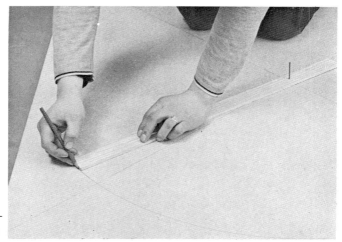

b) marking the circum-
ference of the table top

c) the completed table
use.

A modern sunburst-design wallpaper brightens one wall of a room and makes an interesting focal point above a plain fireplace.

"Flash", which is very simple to use and gives first-class results. All this may sound like splitting hairs, but the job's final appearance depends more than anything else upon careful preparation, and paint won't stick on a greasy or dirty surface.

Preparing the walls With the woodwork thoroughly clean, next give an eye to the wall-paper. If it is torn anywhere, paste back the flaps, and if it has come away from the wall in blisters, *tear* the blister carefully from one end to produce a flap and then paste as before. Do not cut, but tear the paper, for a cut edge will show through whatever paint you will be using.

Then smooth down any irregularities in the wall-paper, using a fine glass-paper. Take care not to rub too hard and work in spirals rather than in straight lines. When this has been done, wipe the walls with a *slightly* damp cloth to remove any dust produced from the sanding down.

If the wall-paper is too badly torn, bubbled, or so heavily embossed that it would look ugly if painted, then it will have to be stripped. Stripping

Figure 1. Preparing a wall for papering. 1, All cracks should be filled. 2, Small narrow cracks should be opened into a 'V' shape to hold the new plaster. 3, Fill cracks with a cellulose-plaster filler. 4, Sand down flush with existing plaster.

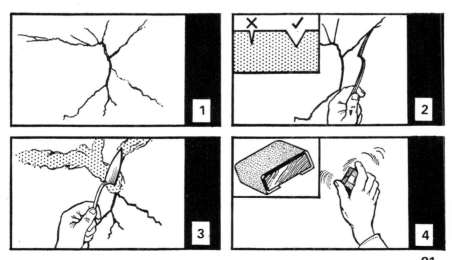

Figure 2. How to 'cut-in' using a piece of
thin cardboard.

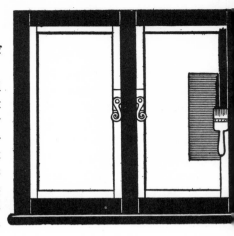

off wall-paper is tremendous fun, and
if not varnished, very easy—but
beware: don't do it unless absolutely
necessary. *It is very difficult to re-
paper a wall properly.* Assuming that
this is necessary and the paper has
been removed, any cracks in the
plaster must be filled as Fig. 1, and
irregularities sanded down. Then
expert assistance must be enlisted to
help with the repapering—it is almost impossible to do it by yourself.

Painting the woodwork All is now ready for the painting to commence,
and the woodwork should be tackled first, using any good quality paint,
preferably oil-bound. It is worth giving some thought to the colour
scheme so that the walls and paintwork harmonize or contrast with each
other and with the other colours in the room. Making little drawings of
your room and painting them with various combinations of colour can
often give you an idea as to what will be the best scheme.

Always clean the window-panes before painting the frames. This is
because the new paint takes several weeks to dry really thoroughly, and
any attempt to clean the windows too soon after painting may result in
the paint getting scuffed.

When you open the tin be sure to give the paint a thoroughly good
stirring with a clean splinter of wood and keep stirring at intervals during
the painting if you want the whole job to appear the same shade. Then
take a one-inch brush of good quality—poor, cheap brushes don't pay.
The hairs come out and spoil the job. Start painting from the top,
"cutting-in" at the sides of doors and windows and around the picture
rail and skirting-board, wiping each part of the woodwork with a *slightly*
damp cloth just beforehand.

"Cutting-in" is the term used to describe painting along a line or an
edge so that none of the paint runs over or gets on the adjacent surface;

82

between a wall and a door-frame or between the skirting-board and the floor are examples of where you " cut-in ". All good decorators cut-in and you should follow their example. A steady hand and a little patience are all that is needed.

To make cutting-in easier try to buy or borrow a sash-brush which is made especially for the job. Some people try to avoid cutting-in by using a piece of thin card or tin as shown in Fig. 2 but this encourages bad workmanship and is not to be practised, unless you haven't a fine brush.

If when cutting-in round window-panes any spots of paint get on to the glass, wait until these have dried hard and then scrape them off with a razor blade.

When picture-rail and skirting-board are finished, wedge the door and paint its various parts in the order shown in Fig. 3. Then commence the window-frames, painting around the glass first and again working from top to bottom and from left to right. Allow 24 hours to elapse between applying the undercoat and the top coat.

Painting the walls At least twelve hours must now be given whilst the paint dries hard, and then a start can be made on the walls, using an oil-bound distemper or an emulsion paint, and a roller. Note that the wall-paper should *not* be sized before painting. Always use the paint as directed on the tin; for example, two coats of emulsion should always be given, the first coat being diluted with half water and the top coat being applied full-strength. However, to produce a good tidy job, more is needed than paint and a roller, so here are a few tips.

When you purchase a paint roller you will also be given a special tray that goes with it, and into which paint must be poured (after ten minutes of steady stirring) up to the marked line. The tray is arranged on a tilt, so that the paint remains at its lower end. The paint roller, which is covered with soft woollen fabric or foam rubber, should first be soaked in warm water and rolled on a clean flat surface until almost all the water is removed. Then roll it from the upper end of the tray down into the paint, doing this a few times to pick up the paint at three or four points on the roller; then roll it to and fro on the upper end of the tray until the roller is evenly coated. This is important. Now to the wall.

83

Painting a door

Figure 3. This drawing shows the correct order for painting a door and the direction of the brush strokes.

How to paint with a roller   Start rolling the paint on at a left-hand corner down by the skirting-board and move the roller slowly upwards to the picture-rail, maintaining a steady, even pressure all the time. (Fig. 4, A.) Then reload the roller and do stroke 2, (4, B) slightly overlapping 1 following up with stroke 3, (Fig. 4, B) which should overlap the other two.

Now, *without* reloading the roller, roll a criss-cross pattern (4, 5, 6, and 7) over 1, 2, and 3, to even out any irregularities before repeating the three painting strokes to link up with the first three.   It is very important

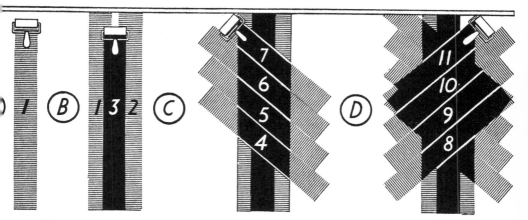

Figure 4.   A roller should be used in up and down and criss-cross movements.

that the criss-crossing is done after every third painting stroke, because, if the work is done in warm weather or the room is warm, the paint, being partly absorbed by the wall-paper, dries very quickly and cannot be evened out at a later stage.

Repeat this sequence until the whole wall-side is finished, then, before tackling another wall, touch in along the vertical corners, picture-rail and skirting-board with a small brush, not overlapping the main body of the work more than necessary.   As the first wall will finish at a corner, when touching in here, the first corner of the adjoining wall can also be touched in and the roller-painting started from this point—still working from bottom to top and from left to right.

Finishing off

Care should be taken at all times to ensure that as little paint as possible gets on the floor. Oil-bound paint should be wiped up immediately with rag dipped in turps, and drips of emulsion paint must be completely removed *at once* with a wet rag. Once dry it is very difficult to remove emulsion paint from the floor or anywhere else where it is not wanted. However, apart from the odd drip, paint splashes are only a sign of carelessness and it usually means that you have too much paint on your brush or roller. Any drips that get missed whilst you are working can be shifted more often than not with some wire wool and elbow-grease.

Finishing off and cleaning up Do not be unduly disappointed if the wall when finished looks patchy or of different shades. The former will disappear when the distemper or emulsion is quite dry and the latter is due .only to the position of the walls with respect to reflected light from the window. Do not worry either if the paper detaches itself from the wall at places when wetted by the distemper. As the latter dries, the paper will go taut again and the blisters disappear. The lock and finger-plates from the door should be carefully cleaned and then given two coats of paint before being refixed. When the job is finished the paint-roller must be thoroughly soaked and washed in warm water until every trace of distemper or emulsion has disappeared, after which it should be hung by its handle until dry. Never store the roller in any other position than that of hanging by its handle. Clean paint brushes as described on page 77.

It is a good idea to put a little of each kind of the paint you have used in small jars and seal them tightly, then you'll have on hand paint for touching-up should you need to at any future time.

Brightening up
your room—or pad

Not everyone can afford to re-decorate their room completely, but here are some ideas which may help to give it quite a 'new look'.

Useful Lamps   Fig. 1, 1, shows a wooden angle lamp which can be moved into almost any position.   This is simple to make, and the movement is obtained by butterfly bolts at the three joints; these are tightened when you have obtained the angle you desire.   The wire and lamp-holder need to be bought specially, but, with a little ingenuity, the shade can be made at home.   The wood can be either painted, stained or waxed.

The other reading lamp, suitable for fitting to a *tall*, bed-headboard, is also easily made.   The light source is a small, fluorescent tube.   The ends of the shade are made from two triangular pieces of wood, rounded at the apex.   These will be joined together by the tube, but strips of wood can be fitted along the bottom of the shade for additional strength.   Providing the frame for the shade is strong enough, almost any material can be used for the covering.   The brackets (Fig. 1, 4) can either be fixed to the end-pieces or to a wooden batten joining them.

The shade in Fig. 1, 5, is made to revolve by the heat of the lamp, and the pattern that is punched on the paper shade is projected on to the walls so that it revolves with it!   Here is how it works.   Good balance is vital, so either buy a suitable metal frame or make one very carefully as in Fig. 1, 6.   The only point of contact between the shade and lamp-base is at the apex of the cone attached to the bulb.   This can be carved from wood and fixed to the bulb with stiff wire as shown.   The shade is made to revolve by fitting two vanes (Fig. 1, 7) at opposing angles.   The heat from the lamp strikes these, and propels the entire shade slowly round.   To prevent the shade wobbling, a wire can be taken across the bottom of the frame, encircling—but not touching—the stem of the lamp.

87

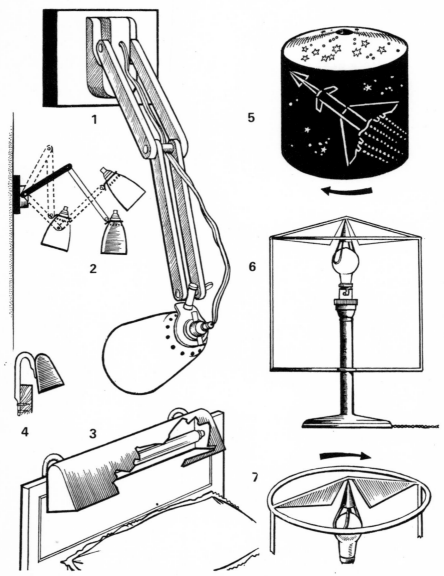

Figure 1. Ideas for a desk light, bed light, and a table lamp with a revolving shade.

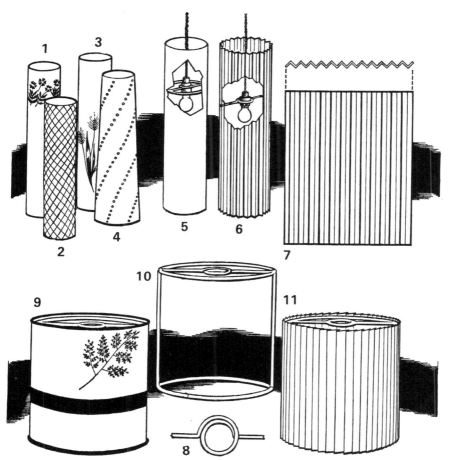

Figure 2. Here are a number of attractive easily-made lampshades.

Making Lampshades Fig. 2, 1-6, are made from thick paper and need no metal frame, except for a support for the bulb as shown in Fig. 2, 5, and 6. The support shown in Fig. 2, 6, can be easily made as shown in Fig. 2, 8. Fig. 2, 6, and 7 show how a corrugated shade is made. The paper must be thick and is scored with a back of a knife and a ruler. Fig. 2, 9-11, show larger shades, Fig. 2, 10, being the frame required. For a

Figure 3. How to block in a fireplace, and ideas for indoor plants and gardens.

really attractive result pieces of grass can be dried, painted in bright colours and stuck to the paper of the shade, as in Fig. 2, 9.

Other useful ideas Fig. 3, 1 and 2 show how an old fireplace, no longer used, can be blocked-in with hardboard, nailed to battens to keep it flat, and painted. A large photograph or coloured print can be fixed to it to

90

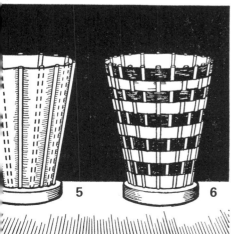

brighten up the surface. Plants help to make any room attractive—Fig. 3, 3 and 4 show an idea for a shelf of plants. The shelf is made from dowelling, and a piece of plain coloured cloth is stretched over a board and mounted against the wall. Mounting small pots of cacti on to peg-board, as shown in Fig. 3, 5 and 6, makes a compact wall garden. The pots are held in place by looping a piece of thickish wire around them, pushing it through a hole in the board, and twisting the wire into a knot. The tray at the bottom of the board catches any drips of water or earth, and can be made from sheet tin or plywood. Paint the peg-board a light colour to throw the pots into relief. As the weight of the pots may be heavier than you think, fix the peg-board to the wall at four points using Rawlplugs and long screws. Wooden blocks between the board and the wall will improve the appearance of the fixture.

Each of the six styles of waste-paper basket shown in Fig. 4 have the same base, a circular piece of wood made about 1 in. thick. In styles 1, 2, and 3, thick paper is wrapped around the outside and decorated. Styles 4, 5, and 6, show the same base with pieces of dowel embedded $\frac{1}{2}$ in. into the base. Material, paper or raffia can then be plaited between them, or the basket can be left plain as in style 4.

Figure 4. Suggestions for smartly designed waste-paper baskets you can make yourself.

Lending a hand in the garden

There are plenty of useful jobs for the handy boy to do in the garden. Just take a walk round and see what can be done.

Building a concrete bird-bath   A concrete bird-bath is not quite the complicated job one might imagine.   The centre post and the basin itself may be made quite easily by casting cement or concrete in appropriate moulds as shown in Fig. 1.

First, the mould is made for the pillar by cutting four pieces of $\frac{1}{2}$ in.-thick wood to the sizes shown and nailing them together strongly.   Care must be taken to ensure that the inside surfaces are smooth and without nails, otherwise the mould will be difficult to remove from the concrete when it has set.   Next, the actual bath is moulded by using two plastic hand bowls of appropriate sizes to produce a casting of sufficient thickness to be strong (Fig. 1, 3 and 4).

Now to the making of the concrete, which should be mixed dry in the proportions of one of cement, three of washed sand, and two of small pebbles or finely broken bricks.   If pebbles or broken bricks are not available, a substitute is the finely graded coke which is used in domestic kitchen boilers.   The ingredients must be well mixed before adding enough water to make a fairly stiff paste.   You should not attempt to do this job during frosty or icy weather as the water in the concrete may freeze and crack the concrete whilst it is setting.

The inside of the pillar mould is now lined with newspaper, or well oiled with motor engine oil, and is stood upside-down on a level surface; after which the concrete is poured inside it and rammed down as filling proceeds to ensure that the mass is free from air bubbles.   This ramming-down is very important.   A piece of iron pipe can be added for strength.

Now take two short lengths of thick dowel or broomstick handle and

92

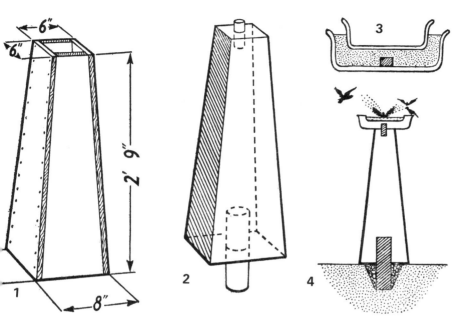

Figure 1. **Plans showing how a concrete bird-bath can be made.**

grease them well. Press them into the centre of the ends of the pillar, one at each end, until nothing projects above the surface of the cement. Then leave the mould upright for 24 hours until the cement is set hard.

While setting is taking place, the actual bath can be made by oiling the inside and outside of the plastic bowls and filling with concrete to the rim of the lower basin. Before filling, however, an inch-long piece of broomstick must be placed centrally on the bottom of the larger basin to produce a hole in the casting into which a spigot will be fitted later to prevent the cast basin from being moved on top of the pillar. Allow 24 hours for the concrete to set.

The wooden moulding is then removed from the cast pillar and a wood-screw driven into the end of each of the pieces of broomstick, by which they can be carefully withdrawn, leaving holes in the casting. Similarly, the outer plastic basin is bent away to reveal the basin casting, the wooden

93

block removed, and the inner basin extracted. With this done, allow another 24 hours for the concrete to set off really hard.

Finally, cut two more lengths of broomstick, paint well with creosote, and drive one into each hole in the pillar, allowing about 6 in. to project at the bottom and about 1 in. at the top. The projection will fix the pillar to the ground where desired and lock the basin position at the top of the pillar, whilst allowing it to be removed for cleaning. If desired, the whole structure may be coloured by using coloured cement, which may be purchased; an attractive shade is dark green.

Making a tool-rack Another easily-made garden accessory which is very useful is the tool-rack illustrated in Fig. 2, which is almost self-explanatory. A piece of board about one inch in thickness should be used, and the hooks made from short lengths of dowel-rod and broomstick, or 6 in. French nails.

Making a thatched bird-house The interest and appearance of the most 'ordinary' garden can be greatly improved by the addition of a simply-designed bird-house, which can be erected near a window, so that during the quiet winter months our feathered visitors can be watched whilst they

Figure 2. A home-made tool-rack such as this could be lengthened to include many more tools.

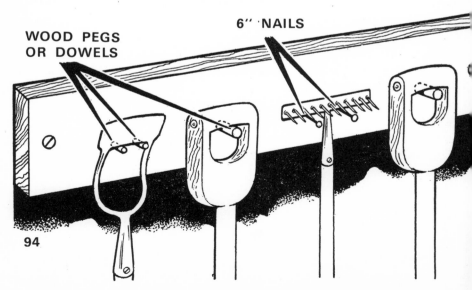

WOOD PEGS
OR DOWELS

6" NAILS

eat in perfect safety from feline marauders. Such a bird sanctuary is described here, the construction of which is simple in the extreme yet intriguing because it boasts a thatched roof.

First a six-foot length of timber is required for the main post, and this may be a section cut from a tree-trunk or branch providing its diameter is somewhere in the region of four inches. At least eighteen inches of this post should be buried in the ground and the hole dug to receive it should not be made larger than necessary, so that the post may be firmly wedged in place with rammed-down stones. Cement and sand made into concrete may be used if desired.

For the floor of the house a disc of wood about fifteen inches in diameter must be cut from material about one inch thick. Dimensions are not important, but strength and general proportion should be studied. If an old table-lamp shade is available it will be unnecessary to make up the conical wire frame shown in Fig. 3, otherwise the frame should be roughly constructed from 16 S.W.G. galvanized iron wire, the joints being twisted together with pliers. Here again great accuracy is unnecessary.

Three half-inch holes must now be drilled through the floor where shown to take the uprights, each of which consists of a 10 inch length of half-inch dowel-rod, which is driven into the appropriate hole after a small hole has been drilled to receive the lower hoop of the wire roof-frame.

With the framework of the house finished, thatching can commence—an interesting yet straightforward job in which the materials used consist of good stiff grass or hay, bound down to the framework with fine galvanized wire or good string.

First prepare long bundles of the grass or hay about twice as long as the length from the top of the coned roof to three inches below the lower wire hoop. Get all the stalks lying parallel by gently pulling the bundle through the hands or combing with a large-toothed stable comb, then lay it on the roof with its upper end protruding well above the top of the cone roof. Secure the upper end temporarily in place with a rubber band and the lower end to the lower wire hoop, and continue round the roof until it is completely covered.

Now replace the rubber band with a couple of turns of the finer

95

Making a bird-house

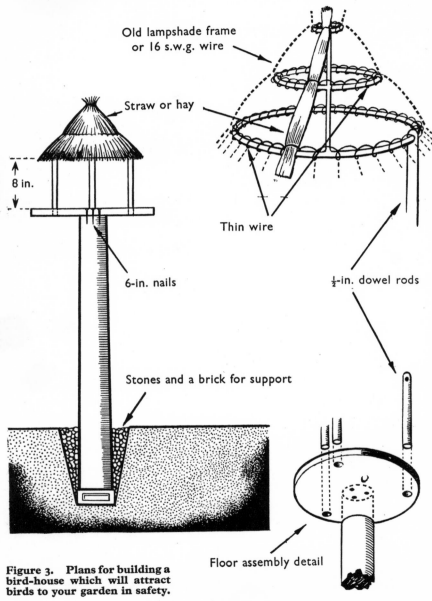

Old lampshade frame or 16 s.w.g. wire

Straw or hay

8 in.

Thin wire

6-in. nails

$\frac{1}{2}$-in. dowel rods

Stones and a brick for support

Floor assembly detail

Figure 3.   Plans for building a bird-house which will attract birds to your garden in safety.

The Council of Industrial Design

A cheerful and practical teenager's study-bedroom with plenty of storage space in the cupboards. The one dark wall makes an effective background to posters and drawings etc.

Three modern lampshades: *left,* made in coloured foil pasted onto card with cut-outs; *centre,* with circles of foil pasted onto wire; *right,* using folded and slatted coloured card.

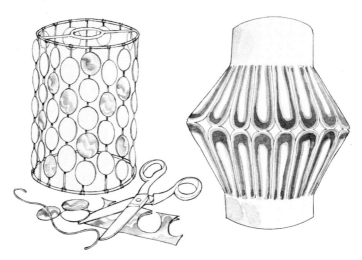

(*above*) A garden pool is fun to make and will give hours of pleasure when it is stocked with a variety of fish, plants and other water-life.

Cement and Concrete Association

Stanley Works (Great Britain) Ltd.

(*right*) Crazy paving makes almost any garden look better. It is well worth the effort involved to achieve the deceptively 'crazy' effect.

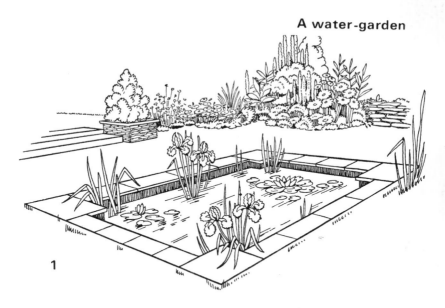

A water-garden

1

Figure 4. One of the loveliest things you can make is a garden pond. The materials for a pool as large and deep as this would cost several pounds, and its construction would need many hours of work. For these reasons you would need to obtain the help of an older member of the family. But there is no reason why you should not build a smaller, shallower pond yourself.

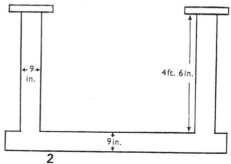

2

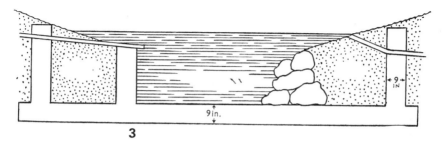

3

galvanized wire and also take a long wire stitching through the thatch to secure it to the middle loop to give additional strength and to prevent the thatch being blown off in the winter.

If desired a bird-house of this design may be hung with a short length of chain to a tree branch with good effect, whilst regarding the general finish it could well be painted bright colours or creosoted, as desired, to preserve the wood.

Here are two full-scale garden jobs that are great fun to do, but need the assistance of an older member of the family; they would take too long and cost too much to tackle on your own.

Making a garden pool need not be the ambitious task it sounds: there is no reason why you should build one as large or as deep as the delightful

Figure 5. The main stages in laying crazy-paving.

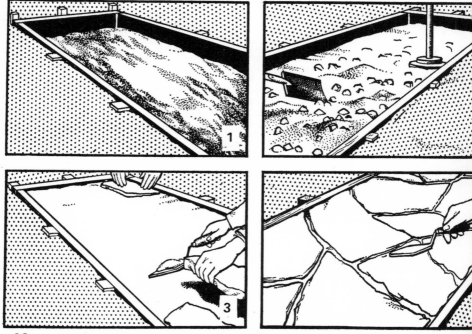

pool shown in Fig. 4, 1. In fact, the easiest pools to make are dish-shaped ones which need be no more than a few inches deep.

Whatever the size, the position of your pool is important. It should not be placed near a large tree, the roots of which may crack the concrete, and an overflow pipe must be fitted to drain away surplus water. Small rock pools should always have a plug to drain water which, in winter, may otherwise freeze and crack the concrete.

The foundations of a large pool should be made from 4 in. of broken bricks, stones, and rubble (called hard-core) and covered with 3 in. of concrete. When the floor has set, the walls are built up, section by section, being held in place by wooden planks (called shuttering) until the concrete has set (see photograph). When this has been done the concrete is covered with a facing of cement 1 or 2 in. thick. Small, dish-shaped pools need be no more than 3 to 4 in. thick altogether.

The concrete for this job should be made from 4 parts of washed ballast, 2 parts of washed sand, and 1 part of cement. The concrete must be rammed well home to prevent air-pockets forming.

How to lay crazy paving Crazy paving is probably the most attractive kind of garden path and is not difficult to lay. First dig a trench about 6 to 9 in. deep, as Fig. 5, 1, and make a firm edge with planks held in place with wooden pegs. Then add broken brick and rubble. Concrete and ram well down (Fig. 5, 2) to about 3 to 4 in. thick; lay 1 to 2 in. of concrete on top of this (Fig. 5, 3). The paving stones are set *into* this and tapped lightly into position. Finish the joints with cement (Fig. 5, 4). Another method is to lay ashes instead of the concrete on top of the rubble, and bed the stones into a layer of sand 1 in. thick. If the path is to be situated against one of the walls of the house, slope the paving and foundations slightly, so that rain water will drain away from the house.

Block printing

Every method of printing employs basically the same technique of transferring an impression from one surface to another through a medium such as ink or dye. This principle applies as much to the printing of a great national newspaper as it does to the making of a simple potato block.

Although most printing techniques are far too complicated and expensive to be practised in the home, block-making and -printing offers considerable scope to the young handicraft worker with limited funds. Block-making, as will be seen from this and the following chapter, is itself varied in technique and application, and even if you do not consider yourself to be a good artist, you will soon find that you can make pleasing designs that can be used to print book jackets, book plates, calendars, box covers, greetings cards, wrapping papers, postcards, programme and magazine covers, fabrics, china, wood and glassware.

Fortunately, the materials and equipment are all easy to obtain, and you can start work at a cost of only a few pence. The easiest of all the block-making techniques is potato printing.

Potato Printing
All that you need for your first attempt at block-making is an ordinary potato and a sharp knife. The diagram (Fig. 1) shows the process in ten stages.

First wash the outside of the potato, and then cut it in half. If you now ink the flat surface of one half and press it firmly on a piece of paper, it will make a solid impression of exactly the same shape (stages 1-3).

With the unused half of the potato you can make your first attempt at cutting away the part that is not to be printed. Hold the half potato

100

so that the cut side is uppermost. Place the knife-edge across the flat surface, tilting the blade towards the left at an angle of about 45 degrees and cut a V-shaped nick (stages 4 and 5).

If you have made these two cuts carefully, you should now be able to remove the triangular-shaped piece cleanly from the surface (stage 6). Your half potato should now look like the one sketched in stage 7, and if you apply ink to its surface and then press it on to a piece of paper, it will make an impression like that in stage 8.

Your next step can be to cut, say, the initial letter of your name. This needs a little more care, as you must be sure to cut only where necessary. Stage 9 shows what the half potato looks like from above when you have marked the outline of the letter "T" on its surface. The shaded portion is the part that must be cut away. Do the actual cutting in exactly the same way as before, always slanting the knife-blade and making the cuts from the top surface downward. Never cut straight down, and never cut under the surface. Then remove the unwanted background by carefully cutting or paring across the potato.

Figure 1. Making a potato cut.

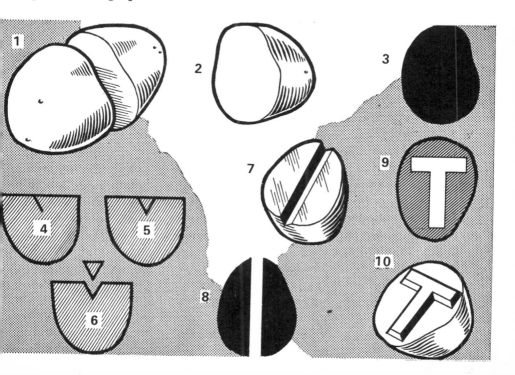

Cutting designs

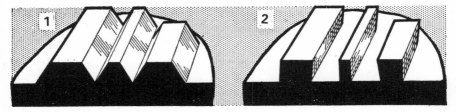

Figure 2. (1) The right and (2) wrong methods of cutting a potato.

Make the cuts round the outside of the letter very carefully and cleanly; it does not matter very much if the "background" surface is a little uneven. The last stage shows what the potato should look like after you have cut away the blackground.

Note that the cut sides of the letters slant outward and so make a firm base, wider than the top surface. Fig. 2 shows the right and wrong methods of cutting.

Cutting Designs The next stage in potato block-making is cutting a small design. First of all draw a design on paper. This design should be simple and bold, as it is impossible to get fine lines or details with potatoes, and you will only waste your time if you try. Much of the charm of a potato print lies in the gently ragged effect it produces, so it is best to choose a design in which this effect can be used to the fullest advantage. Your design might be an informal geometric one like that shown in Fig. 3. Although this design may not look very effective by itself, when it is used as a "unit" in working out a pattern it is really astonishing how good the results can be.

When you have sketched your design on paper, cut a potato in half and then cut out the design in the same way that you cut out the letter. You should get a block like one shown in Fig. 3.

Figure 3. The prepared potato block and the print produced.

102

Printing With potato blocks you can print on paper, cardboard, fabrics, wood, glass, china, and some plastics. You can use almost any kind of ink or paint, provided that it does not dry too quickly.

A pad of blotting-paper (or newspapers) will make a serviceable " bed " for the paper that is to be printed on. A slightly absorbent paper takes the print best. Lay your first sheet of paper on the pad, and prepare your paint or ink. Brush the colour smoothly and evenly on the printing surface of the potato, and then immediately, while the colour is still wet, press the potato firmly on the paper. Remove the printed paper, and place another sheet on the pad. Brush the colour on the printing surface of the potato and print as before. Continue the operation as required. The block must be freshly inked for each print. The colours of the inks can be varied as you proceed with the design.

Stick Printing

Many people claim that printing with pattern sticks is even easier than potato block-printing, and the one great advantage is that the block will last much longer.

Sets of pattern printing sticks (with a wide variety of different patterns) can be bought quite cheaply ready for use. The design on each stick is small, and the idea is to print groups or arrangements to form a complete pattern, using different colours as desired. Most people, however, consider it more enterprising to cut their own blocks. Nevertheless, with only one set of sticks an almost endless variety of patterns can be developed and printed on paper, card, cork, or smooth fabric.

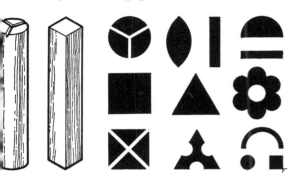

Pattern Designs Fig. 4 shows a few of the stock-pattern sticks that can be

Figure 4. Two printing sticks and some typical stick patterns.

103

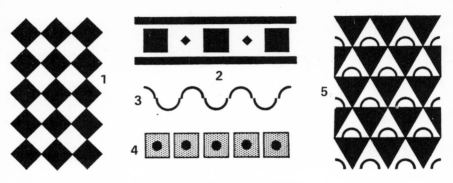

Figure 5. Patterns made with combinations of sticks.

obtained. The simple square can be used to make the chequer-board effect of Fig. 5, 1. The check pattern is the simplest form of what is called the "all-over" pattern. Three different sticks are used to make the formal border (Fig. 5, 2), and a different colour could be used for each one. In Fig. 5, 3 only one stick, the semicircular line, is used to make one continuous undulating line. This is done by "reversing" the pattern for each alternate print. Fig. 5, 4 is a border made with the plain square and small solid circle. Fig. 5, 5 is another "all-over" pattern, made with the triangular section and the semicircular line. This would make an effective book-jacket design if you used a different colour for each of the two blocks.

Poster or water-colours may be used for printing on paper or card. These paints should not be mixed with water, but with a good liquid paste. For printing on fabrics or leather either printer's ink or the special fabric paint should be used.

The method of printing is similar to that for potato blocks. Apply colour to the printing surface, hold the stick in a perfectly upright position, and press it on the material firmly and deliberately. Remove the stick cleanly. When printing on paper or card do not use too great a quantity of paint.

Making your own Pattern Sticks To make your own pattern sticks is not difficult. You can make an endless variety from materials and articles usually considered useless—odd pieces of wood, rodding, light curtain rods, and other everyday articles in the home. The sticks do not have to be made of wood, nor need they be shaped like sticks.

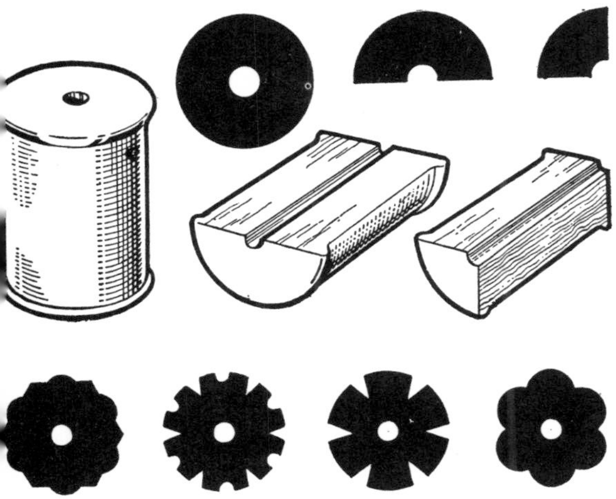

Stick printing

Cotton reels are a natural first choice. You can use a wide range of different sizes without any cutting whatever; it is also very easy to cut or burn patterns into the soft wood. Fig. 6 shows how an ordinary cotton reel can be split into sections, and the shapes that will be printed. The splitting can be done easily with a sharp knife and mallet. Fig. 6 also shows decorative designs that can be obtained from shaping cotton-reel ends by filing, cutting, or burning with a red-hot skewer, and then rubbing smooth with glass-paper.

Figure 6. Printing sticks made from cotton reels and some possible designs.

Rubber sticks Blocks used for printing on soft materials, such as paper and fabrics, make clearer prints when they are hard and resistant. Blocks used for printing on hard surfaces, such as wood, metal and china, should conversely be softer. The best material for surfaces such as these is ordinary india-rubber.

Fig. 7 shows how a pattern can be cut (or burned with a skewer) on a piece of rubber, and the impression that would be made. This diagram also shows the impressions made by other rubber-block patterns.

Cork sticks and other materials Ordinary corks can be used in all sizes and shapes, and produce an interesting grained or mottled effect. The material varies between the hardness of wood and the softness of rubber. You can burn the printing surface with a red-hot needle to produce the design required, or, if cleaner lines are wanted, cut the cork with a razor blade. If the design is burnt on, rub the surface gently with fine glass paper before printing.

Pattern sticks

All kinds of materials can be used for printing and for adding fine details. Wooden skewers are particularly useful for making dots. When sharpened to a point they can be used for dot lettering, and matchsticks can serve for the same purpose. But take great care when adding dots to an existing print, or when making a whole print with dots. Used excessively they can easily produce a fussy or crude result.

Pencils with different shaped sections, preferably with the leads removed, can also be brought in to add finer details to a print. The rims of glasses, boxes, tins, and bottles are all useful for producing regular outlines on occasions. And pieces of net and fabric material, and even the palm of the hand, can provide interesting backgrounds and textures to a print *providing* they are used with restraint and ingenuity.

One of the great joys of block printing is that it provides really enormous possibilities for experimenting with materials and designs. And, if you don't want to, you need never produce the same design twice—although, of course, the whole idea of printing is to be able to reproduce the same design a number of times!

Figure 7. **A rubber block and the kind of impressions that can be obtained with this method.**

Lino cuts

Many people are under the mistaken impression that lino-cutting is a simple, limited craft that is confined to the school art-room. This notion is a long way from the truth and many artists have found lino-cutting a stimulating and sensitive medium of expression. John Farleigh, Julian Trevelyan and John Piper are among the well-known artists who have used lino cuts to produce prints of a very high artistic level. Even the beginner will find that it is possible to produce a range of effects that are as delightful as they are remarkably varied. And with the possibilities provided by the use of colour you will find lino-cutting a demanding and fascinating craft.

It is best to make your first attempts in lino-cutting with as few tools as possible, and then to make and add others only as your improving skill finds them necessary. But in any case a complete linocraft set is not unduly expensive.

Materials Modern inlaid lino or lino that has a glazed surface is useless for block-making. Cork lino can be used but is rather brittle. The old-fashioned plain brown lino (sometimes backed with hessian) is very good, and you can sometimes get off-cuts quite cheaply from a local furnisher's. Artist supply shops and most good stationers sell linoleum especially for block-making.

Tools Although you can cut lino blocks with a sharp penknife, it is certainly worth investing some ten shillings in a set of special lino-cutting tools. These tools are merely small gouges like pen nibs which fit into a small holder. Fig. 1 illustrates a small set containing two V-shaped gouges, two U-shaped gouges and two types of holder. The diagram also shows the type of cut made by each gouge. The V gouges

Cutting tools

are used for cutting outlines or narrow lines, and the U gouges for cutting away unwanted background.

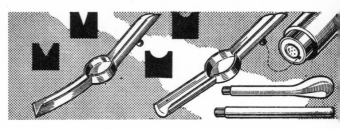

Figure 1. Mitchell's lino-cutting tools, showing the type of cut they make.

Cutting The special advantage of lino for blocks is that it makes it possible to get much finer lines, and a wider range of tones, than with most other materials. However, lino is a comparatively soft material which gives under pressure, and you must, therefore, not make your cuts too close together or leave narrow isolated ridges. As with potato cuts, you must not undercut the printing surface, but should support it by a bank like an inverted letter V.

It is best to start work by taking a piece of lino and practising cutting with the various tools. Fig. 2 shows some of the effects you can attempt.

Most beginners find difficulty in making smooth curves and circles. This difficulty is easily overcome. The secret is to hold the tool firmly in the right hand and move the lino with a smooth, even, circular movement of the left hand. In other words, you hold the tool stationary and guide the lino on to the cutting edge.

The Design There are, broadly speaking, two main types of design: pattern and pictorial. Pattern designing has already been discussed under block printing (page 102). This part, therefore, will deal mainly with the pictorial type of design (Fig. 3).

There are four definite styles: black silhouette on white ground; white silhouette on black ground; white outline on black ground; and black line, with light, shade, and perspective effects.

Figure 2. Practice cuts in lino.

Figure 3. The four basic styles that can be produced with lino cuts.

A simple monogram or silhouette is probably the easiest type of design to start with. A house, tree, ship, bird, or letter may be used.

Transferring the Design When you have decided on your design, draw it out very carefully on paper to the same size and exactly as you want it to appear, but in reverse.

If you want to avoid reversing it is best to draw your design on thin paper and then turn it over and, if necessary, pencil heavily over the outline on the back. Now you can trace the design on to the lino.

There are several other methods of transferring the design to the lino. You can draw it on the lino with pencil or with Indian ink, or you can cover the lino with a wash of white water-colour and then make a tracing on the wash when it is dry.

An excellent way to start is illustrated in Fig. 4, 1. Place a sheet of carbon paper face downward on the lino, and lay the drawing over this. Pin both sheets of

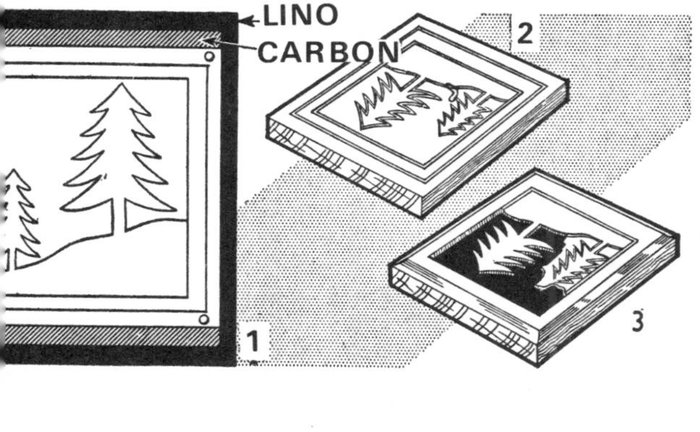

Figure 4. Cutting the block.

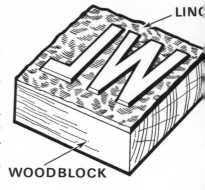

LINO

WOODBLOCK

Figure 5. Lino cut mounted on a wood block.

paper firmly to the lino with drawing-pins, and trace over the drawing in the usual way. Remove the pins and papers, and a carbon tracing of the design should be visible on the lino surface. The carbon lines are easily smudged, and it is a good idea to ink them over, preferably with Indian ink.

Cutting the Block   With one of the V gouges (No. 2 for preference) cut a fairly deep trench all round the outline of the design (Fig. 4, 2).   Then cut away all the ground work with one of the U gouges (Fig. 4, 3).

Printing   When you are printing lino cuts with a printer's press you must mount each cut on a block of wood (as in Fig. 5) to make it the same height as the type.   For pattern printing also, the cut should be mounted on wood, to make it easy to handle.

Ink the lino cut in the way described on page 103.   Then drop a sheet of paper gently on the lino cut, and lay a piece of stiffer paper or card over this.   Rub this firmly with a clean roller, spoon, toothbrush handle, or similar implement.

When pressing on the back of the paper you must be careful not to force the paper out of position.   Before you remove it from the block you can lift a corner with one hand to see whether the ink has taken well and whether enough pressure has been applied.   When satisfactory, peel the print off with a smooth movement that does not drag it across the block.

Printing on fabrics
Lino blocks can be used for printing on fabrics, and linen, muslin, silk and fine cotton are the most suitable.   For printing on fabrics the colour must not be merely applied to the surface: it must be impregnated right into the fibres of the material itself (Fig. 6).

The finer-woven fabrics, such as linen, muslin, and silk are most suitable for block printing.   Rinse the material to be used in hot soapy

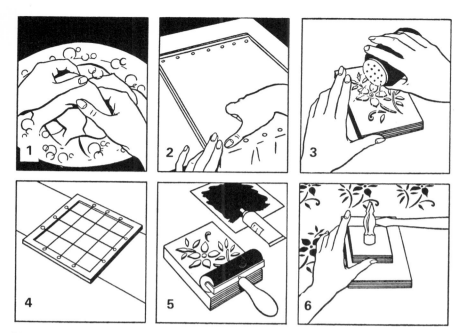

Figure 6. The method for printing on fabrics.

water (stage 1); dry, and iron. Next pin the material tautly over a pad (stage 2). You can make this pad by stretching a blanket tightly over a large pastry-board and covering it with a rubber sheet.

Small patterns can be printed on fabrics in the same way as stick-patterns, but for larger patterns the block should be "flocked". For this you clean the printing surface of the block and lightly cover it with a flocking mordaunt, which is a kind of adhesive. While this adhesive is still wet, sprinkle or dust it with flocking powder (stage 3). Flocking powder is wool in powder form, and by adhering to the sticky mordaunt it makes an absorbent printing surface. This surface must hold sufficient colour to impregnate the material thoroughly, and it usually needs a second application after the first has dried. Each application of mordaunt and flock needs about twenty-four hours to dry. After drying, lightly brush off the surplus flock.

The material may need some guide-lines to indicate where the designs are to be printed. You can make light pencil marks on the material; or, better still, you can make a light frame (stage 4). An old picture frame is easily adapted for the purpose. The guide-lines are made by tying or winding thread round pins which have been set at suitable spaces, and move the frame along the material as required.

Ink the printing surface of the block from the colour prepared on a piece of glass (stage 5), and place the block face down on the material where it is to be reproduced. Firmly tap the wood mount of the block (which is uppermost) with a hammer (stage 6). Remove the block cleanly from the fabric and apply the ink for the next print. When you have completed the printing, allow it to dry. Lightly wash the fabric in warm water and iron before use.

Letters in Lino For printing white on a black ground, single-stroke letters made with the V gouge are easiest, although narrow cuts tend to clog with ink. A more forceful effect is obtained by cutting bolder uprights. The beginner should not be too ambitious with lettering. It always looks so much easier than it actually is.

There is one rule that must always be followed: all letters must be made in reverse. Words must be spelt back to front: thus the first letter of a word will always start from the right of the cut. Fig. 7 shows the letters of the alphabet and figures in reverse and it is a useful guide.

Colour printing Beautiful and tremendously varied results can be obtained with colour printing from lino blocks. The methods range from the very simple to the surprisingly complicated.

A colour print is made by printing two or more blocks on exactly the same area. You need a block for each colour to be used. Always print

Figure 7. The " reversed " alphabet and numerals.

ABCDEFGHIJKL
MNOPQRSTUV
WXYZ 1234567890

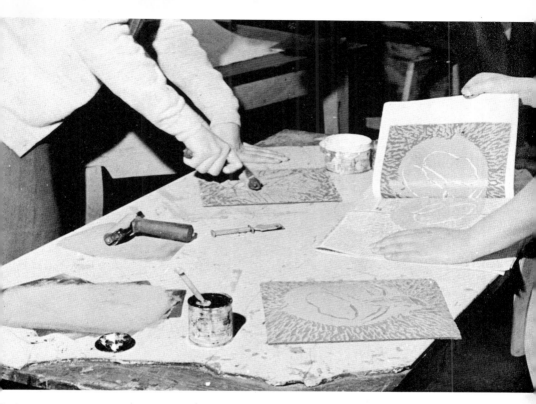

(*above*) A wide choice of block-printing techniques can be used to produce book jackets, book plates, programme covers and printed fabrics.

Teachers World

(*right*) Lino cutting is a rewarding craft which requires care and attention to detail. A lino print such as this one looks good when used on Birthday, Christmas and gift cards.

Reeves and Sons Ltd.

Potato cuts are the most simple printing meth
ods but some of the patterns to be made from
them look very professional and can be quite
intricate.
(*see below*).

Teachers World

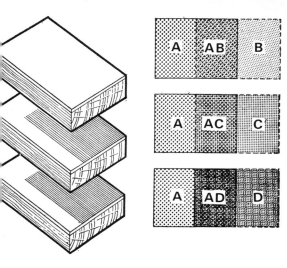

Figure 8. Making a colour and shade chart.

the lightest colour first, then overprint with the next lightest shade, and so on, overprinting the darkest colour last. Great care is needed in designing, cutting and printing to ensure that the right parts and the edges of each of the blocks always come in exactly the right place. This is called getting an accurate "register".

. Before starting on this work, prepare a colour and shade chart (Fig. 8). Cut and mount a few rectangular pieces of smooth lino. Then, on a piece of cartridge or other paper, print a number of these rectangles all in one colour (A). Now apply one sample of each of your other colours (B, C and D) over half of each of the rectangles, producing the shades AB, AC and AD.

Fig. 9 shows how to design a simple colour print. First analyse the complete print by colours (4). You can get the white space (representing snow on the mountains) by using the white of the paper, so you must cut this out on all the blocks making the picture. This leaves three colours—blue, green and yellow. Blue and yellow are primary colours, and green is obtained by mixing them together. So you need only two blocks: one to print yellow (2) and the other to print blue (3). Note that you get the green of the trees and foreground by printing the blue over the yellow.

First make a master outline of the complete picture (1) reducing the picture to its simplest outline. On this outline use coloured pencils or crayons to show the colours in which each part is to be printed. Then take two blocks of exactly the same size, and transfer the appropriate parts of the design to each. Note that only the outlines of the parts to be cut away need be marked; the mountains, for example, need not be

113

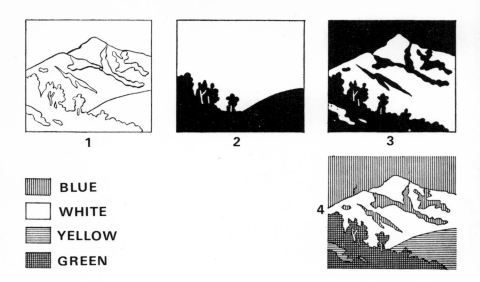

BLUE
WHITE
YELLOW
GREEN

Figure 9. Making a colour-print.

transferred to the block that will print yellow. It is most important, however, to mark the transfer on both blocks so that the parts will make a perfect "fit" when they are overprinted.

The last block to be printed—in this case the blue—is called the key block, and must be cut first. Before cutting your second block, make quite sure that it will make a perfect fit with your key block.

One of the simplest and most effective methods of obtaining an accurate register is to use a frame press (Fig. 10). You can easily make this at home. You need a smooth flat board for the base and two thin strips of wood (of the same thickness as the block or slightly less) which you screw, glue, or tack at right angles to each other. When you print, lightly pin the paper to one of these strips (top or side—it does not matter which) and fold it backward. Then ink the first block with the rubber roller, and set it firmly into the angle. Bring the paper

Figure 10.   A simple frame-press that can be made at home.

114

forward and drop it on the block, press, and then lift. Ink the second block, insert in the angle, and again bring the paper over and press. This completes the printing of a two-colour block. Carefully inspect the print for any flaws that can be corrected before carrying on.

Designing for lino-cutting has its own problems, some of which have been covered in the previous paragraphs on colour. The important thing is to remember its main limitation: it is *very* difficult to include fine detailing in the design. Try to bear this in mind, for you will only be disappointed with the resulting print if you ignore it. The bold clear line is the effect to aim for, but there is no reason why boldness should not be subtle at the same time. If you remember this and the general principles of design laid out on page 108, you will not go far wrong.

Advanced work Lino-cutting and the simpler forms of block-printing, described in the previous chapter, are only two of several methods of printing designs and illustrations open to the craftworker and artist. Lithography, etching and wood cuts are all printing techniques which possess great possibilities for the talented craftsman. Unfortunately, they are also more complex in execution, and the materials and equipment needed are frequently involved and very expensive, especially in regard to presses. When you have tried your hand successfully in the more advanced use of the lino cut, you may feel that you would like to explore, say, etching or lithography. If you do, it is well worth waiting until you have the time to take an evening course at an art or technical school. There, you will find the expert tuition and correct equipment that are essential if you are to develop your skill and talent in the right way.

A simple lino-cut.

Fretwork

Unfortunately, fretwork is not as popular as it once was. This is a great pity, for not only can it be used to make many useful and attractive objects, but it is fine training for the hand and eye.

Tools and materials Fretwork can be done either by means of a hand-frame or with a treadle machine. The latter is preferable, not only because it allows work to be done more quickly, but also because, in inlaying, and in cutting two pieces of wood together for marquetry, or for similar purposes, the saw is automatically retained in an upright position, or given a slight slant if desired, by means of the tilting-table fixed on the machine.

If a hand-frame is used the tools required for the actual fretsawing are a frame and saws, an Archimedean drill with bits for piercing the holes, a cutting board, and a clamp for fixing the board to the edge of a table or bench. This cutting board is a piece of wood or metal with a V-shaped cut in it, to support both sides of the fretwood when sawing with a frame saw. Such a board can be made by the amateur if so desired, but it is best to buy one.

The best-quality saws should be used, and sizes 00 to 2 are the most useful. The heavier types, denoted by higher numbers, are required for heavy work, while the 000 size is suitable only for cutting thin veneers.

A number of reliable firms specialize in fretwoods, and materials can be ordered prepared for use and of the exact thickness required. Among the coloured woods, mahogany works fairly easily, is strong when made up, and little trouble to join. Cedar is lighter, coarser in grain, and not so strong. Walnut is easy to work and to join, and has a nice appearance. Oak is difficult in working, as a rule, and does not give such pleasing results in fretted work as many of the other woods. Holly is about the

116

silkiest and nicest-looking of the white woods, but, like other white materials, it is very difficult to keep clean, and its appearance is spoilt by varnish. Ebony, to go to the other extreme in colour and texture, is brittle and gritty, and a good many saw-blades are broken on it. Rosewood is generally rather gummy in texture, and joining the pieces after cutting is rather difficult. There are also a number of fancy woods with which the fretworker will soon become familiar.

Owing to the liability of fretted wood to warp and twist, three-ply wood is sometimes used. This is extremely tough and strong, but, if the edges of the work have to show, the effect of using it is scarcely artistic. As a general rule, wood of one-eighth or three-sixteenths of an inch should be used for small, light articles, and a quarter-inch or more for heavier work.

Pasting the design   The usual way of transferring the design to the wood consists in pasting down the design bodily and, after the work is finished, removing the paper with glass-paper. This method is generally recommended, although many fretwork plans give only one set of pieces that often have to be cut in duplicate, triplicate, or more. An even better technique is to transfer the design to the wood with good carbon paper and a stylus, or sharp-pointed pencil, since it gives a cleaner finish.

Drilling   A hole must be drilled in the wood, through which the saw is threaded for each part of the design. This hole, which should be drilled carefully with the Archimedean drill, should be made in the waste part of the wood, and the saw taken up to the edge shown on the design after being threaded in the wood. Do not drill a hole on the line of the design, least of all at a corner; for if you do, the line of the design will have to be over-run in order to take out the traces of the hole. After a little practice it will be found possible to bore the hole just on the waste-wood side of the line, so that a single stroke of the saw will take it on to the line. For inlaying work, however, use the smallest drill-bit that will let your saw through the wood, and make the hole in as inconspicuous a part of the design as possible, exactly on the line of the design; the most acute part of a curve is a good place for the hole. One point to remember is that in boring holes, either for threading the saw in the wood or to admit nails

117

Fretwork tools

A treadle-operated fretsawing machine—for general work this is by far the best type of machine to have.

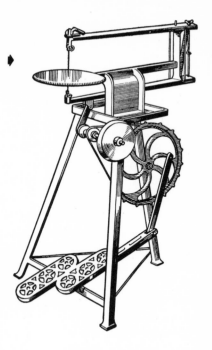

Although an electrically-driven fretsawing machine such as this enables work to be done at high speed, the operator has to be very skilled—otherwise serious errors can be made through not being able to stop the machine in time.

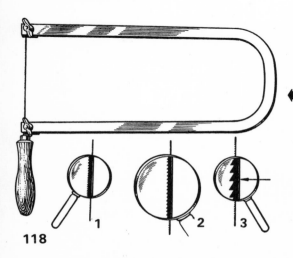

The machines shown above cost many pounds, even when they are bought second hand. For this reason most model makers have to use a hand fretsaw and cutting table. The only disadvantage with a hand saw is that the work takes longer, although many workers prefer this too, because it gives them greater control over the work. Providing the correct blade is used, the fretsaw is useful for cutting a wide range of materials, and not necessarily confined to fretworking.

Blade 1 is fine-toothed and suitable for cutting sheet copper, brass, zinc, vulcanite, bone and horn.

2 is a medium-sized blade for wood, cardboard and plastics.

3 is a strong blade for cutting thick sections and doing heavy types of work.

A pressed-steel cutting table is essential for working with a hand saw.

A modeller's knife with a selection of blades is another very useful fretwork tool.

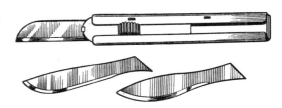

1

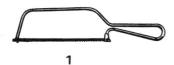

This cigarette box and calendar are two useful articles which can be made by fretwork. There are hundreds of others.

2

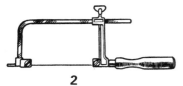

3

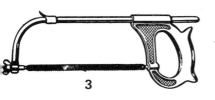

For metal fretwork, hacksaws are basic equipment. Numbers 1 and 3 are necessary for cutting metal in quantity, and number 2 for actually fretting.

119

or screws for fixing, the Archimedean drill should always be used. Any attempt to use a bradawl or gimlet will generally result in cracks and splintering.

Sawing The saw, when fixed, should be strained fairly tightly in the frame—experience will soon determine what degree of straining gives the best result—and in the matter of actual sawing only practice can guide. The main difficulty consists in keeping the saw-blade perfectly upright. Turning the saw in the wood at corners is another difficulty, and can be overcome by moving the saw up and down while turning the wood, the object being not to saw but simply to file the turning-hole large enough to give the saw freedom to move. It is advisable to free-wheel several strokes each time a sharp turn is encountered, otherwise trouble is likely to occur with projecting points, which are apt to snap off if the cutting is not very carefully done.

Inlay and overlay For inlaying and marquetry work a fretsawing machine is a necessity. With this, both hands are free to guide the work up to the saw, and so long as the treadle is worked evenly a machine will do better work than a hand-frame. In inlaying, the table on which the work is done, and through which the saw-blade passes, is slightly tilted, so that the inlay may fit tightly in its bed. The tilting compensates for the amount of wood taken out by the saw. Only a very slight degree of tilting is required; if the table is tilted at too great an angle great pressure will be needed to force the inlay work down into its place after the sawing has been completed. In all fretsawing, work from the delicate parts of the pattern on to the stronger parts, and usually from inside to outside, to avoid breaking the work before fixing is done.

Sawing veneers In sawing veneers for marquetry and inlaying, wood of one-sixteenth of an inch thickness, at the most, should be used. The two pieces, the inlay and the bed in which it is placed, *must* always be fixed together and cut as one. Place a piece of waste wood on top, and if possible underneath as well, as these protect the work while it is in progress and cleaner under-edges to the saw-cuts are obtained, making less glass-papering necessary. For the top surface there should be as little glass-papering as possible, as with a fine-grained and ornamental wood it is difficult to restore a good surface once glass-papering has been started. So far as the design permits, always rub with the grain, and never attempt to use glass-paper except when fixed to a rubber with a flat surface. Any jagged edges may be smoothed with a fretsawing file.

This sort of work ought only to be attempted after considerable practice. Very beautiful effects can be obtained by doing a pattern in, say, holly and rosewood with a machine, and then interchanging the pieces, each whole being glued down on the surface which is to be ornamented, one on each side of the surface. The design is thus produced twice in reverse colours.

Fixing Use good glue, and nails and screws as sparingly as is consistent with the required strength of the work. For box forms of design, the pattern often shows ornamental corners which are made with half-cut-through joints, and these, if accurately sawn, form the best kind of joint for fretwork, though they are rather difficult to glue securely. This makes correct cutting all the more necessary, so that the two pieces may hold each other to a certain extent independently of the glue.

Fretsawing in metal Fretsawing in metal is more difficult than in wood, and it requires special saws and different tools. Some rather good effects can be obtained, but to get a really good finish on any work the file has to be used almost as much as the special metal-cutting fretsaw. In the case of most metals, the work, after finishing, has to be polished with pumice powder and water. In addition to metal-cutting saws, small twist-drills are required for the Archimedean drill-stock, and both drill-point and saw must be kept lubricated with oil while being used. Apart from these things, and the extreme slowness with which the work is done, there is little difference between wood and metal fretsawing.

Bookbinding

In recent years the cost of producing books has risen steeply. One outcome has been that not only are books frequently bound less strongly than they were in the past, but that many really good books are now published as paper-backs. And often these are the only books that young people can afford to buy. Whilst paper-backed books look very attractive when new, they soon become tattered and dog-eared if handled very often.

If you buy paper-backs and want to keep your book shelves looking tidy, the answer is to rebind these books in strong, durable, hard covers. Whilst there is a kit on the market for doing this, it is cheaper and much more stimulating and interesting to tackle the whole job for yourself. You will soon discover that it is not difficult and that the range of possible finishes is truly remarkable. By rebinding paper-backs as soon as they are acquired, you will find that before long your shelves contain well-bound books that are really pleasing and individual in appearance.

There is no reason why your activities should end—or even begin—with paper-backs; rebinding a year's issues of a favourite magazine is another excellent starting point, and with a little experience, rebinding damaged hard-covered books can be tackled, too. Beginning in this way will serve as an admirable introduction to the great and ancient craft of bookbinding.

Materials The choice of materials is wide, and most are easy to obtain. You need boards for the stiff covers, and you can get these in various thicknesses and qualities. Millboard is one of the best, but it is not too easy to cut cleanly. Leatherboard is also good. Strawboard is cheaper and popular for simpler work, but is easily damaged. Pulpboard and cardboards vary considerably in quality, but are rarely as good as strawboard. Thin card can be strengthened by sticking two or more pieces together. The outsides of the boards can be covered with many different materials. The best and most expensive are vellum and leathers (morocco, persian calf, calf, and the humbler skiver). Bookcloths and some imitation leather and fabric cloths are also fairly expensive. Art canvas is good. Bookbinders' linen is perhaps the most suitable for all kinds of simple bookbinding in both strength and price. Hessian and cretonne may be used for certain types of book. Cover papers are quite cheap and are sold in a wide range of qualities, colours and finishes; they are especially useful for smaller books.

The inside surfaces of the boards need to be covered with end-papers. These are fairly thin sheets of paper which you can buy cheaply, either plain or in a choice of colours, patterns, or marbled effects. You can also use ordinary cartridge paper; off-cuts from this are useful for filling in. Other materials required are a little thin muslin (bookbinders' mull for preference); bookbinders' tape; a skein of linen thread and a needle; a ball of hemp threadcord; headbands of either linen or silk; a good paste; and glue (preferably Scotch glue).

Tools and equipment You do not need many tools to make a start with bookbinding. Those that are really necessary are : a pair of sharp scissors; a flexible cutting knife; a ruler (a metal straight-edge is best); a small setsquare; a backing hammer (a Warrington type is excellent); a small tenon saw; and finally a cutting board. Much of the equipment for more advanced work can be made or adapted at home. The most important articles are a sewing press and a cutting (or laying) press, each complete with a pair of backing and cutting boards.

How a book is made up If you examine a book you will find it is made up of a number of sections, each of which is made from one large sheet. When a sheet has been folded only once (making two leaves to the section) it is called folio. Folded twice (four leaves) it is quarto, or 4to; folded three times (eight leaves) it is octavo, or 8vo; and folded four times (sixteen leaves) it is sexto decimo, or 16mo. As a rule a small letter or figure is printed at the bottom left-hand corner of the first page of each

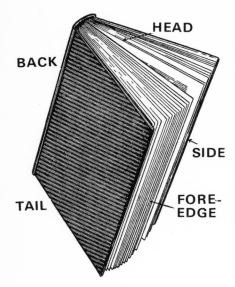

BACK

HEAD

SIDE

FORE-
EDGE

TAIL

Figure 1. Technical names for the various
parts of a book.

section of a book. The letters or figures are consecutive; thus the first three sections of a book are usually lettered A, B and C, or numbered 1, 2 and 3. These indicators are called "signatures", and their purpose is to help the binder to bind the sections of the book in their correct order. Assembling the sections together is called collating. The technical names of the different parts of a book are shown in Fig. 1 and will be used where appropriate.

Preparing and collating the sections   A good way to start bookbinding is to rebind a book of moderate size. First remove the cover and then cut the old thread free and gently pull it out. It is best to use your fingers to remove the old glue remaining on the back of the sections, but you may need a knife for the more obstinate pieces. Carefully clean all the sections of the book.

Alternatively, you can bind together a year's issues of your favourite magazine or periodical. In this case it is best to start with a slim periodical, in which each part can be considered as a complete section. Usually you will find that each section is held together with one or two wire staples. Open the section at the middle, and you will see the ends of the staples. Prise them up gently, and carefully draw the staples out from the outside. Next remove the outside cover and any advertisement pages from the beginning and the end of the section. Do this to each section in turn, and then mark the signatures in consecutive order in the left-hand margin of each section. Finally flatten out any folded sheets or turned-down corners, and trim the edges if necessary.

Simple sewing   Sew each section with needle and thread as shown in Fig. 2, 1 and tie two ends on the inside with a reef knot. When you have

124

sewn each section in this way, place the sections in their correct order on top of one another, with the outside edges in exact alignment. Then sew loops of thread vertically through the sections at each horizontal loop (Fig. 2, 2); make each of these loops with a separate piece of thread, and tie the ends together. For a stronger bind, glue two tapes round the back of the sections but inside the stitching (Fig. 2, 3); allowing 1 to $1\frac{1}{2}$ in. of each tape to project above and below. When the binding is complete the ends of the tapes will be stuck between the boards and the end-papers.

End-papers Take two folded sheets, and paste one with a narrow strip of thick paste ($\frac{1}{8}$ to $\frac{1}{4}$ in. wide) to the inside of the other fold (Fig. 3, 1). To make sure that this strip of paste is of uniform width, mask the paper on each side of the strip with waste paper or card and hold firmly as you apply the paste. Press the pasted part tightly, and let it set under pressure. Take two more folded sheets, and prepare another set of end-papers in the same way. Place the end-papers round the book as in Fig. 3, 2, paste on to the inside of the first and last pages of the book, carefully mark where the fore-edge of the book aligns with them, and trim the end-papers to book size.

Simple binding Cut two pieces of strawboard of exactly the same size.

Figure 2. Sewing a small multi-section book.

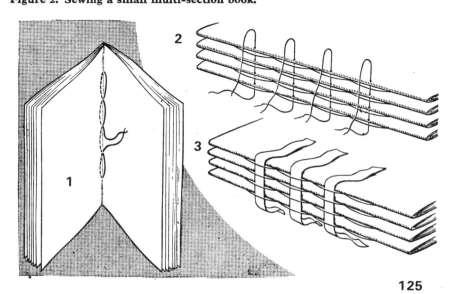

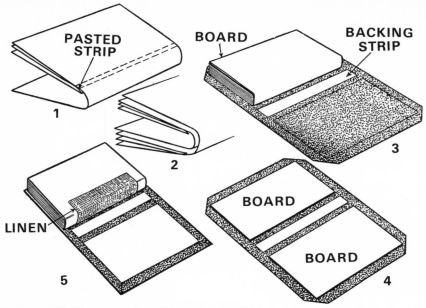

Figure 3. Binding a small multi-section book.

They should be about the same width as the page of the book, but about
$\frac{1}{4}$ in. deeper. Place both pieces of board on a flat surface, and lightly
pencil initials to indicate back, head, fore-edge, and tail. Now draw light
guide-lines on the inside of each board about $\frac{1}{8}$ in. from the outer edges.
When the boards are fitted to the book, the end-papers should just touch
these lines. Next cut a piece of cloth, or whatever material you intend
using, large enough to cover the back and both sides, and to project at
least $\frac{1}{2}$ in. all round. Measure and cut off the corners evenly, and lay the
cloth face down on the table. Place the boards on the cloth so that the
fore-edges are about $\frac{1}{2}$ to $\frac{3}{4}$ in. from the edge of the cloth, and carefully
mark guide-lines on the cloth. Cut a piece of *thin* card to the width of
the back of the sections and of the same length as the boards. This is the
backing strip. Place it in its position (see Fig. 3, 3), mark this on the
covering cloth, and take the backing strip off the cloth again. Now place
a dab of paste in the middle of each board (on the face, which will be on
the inside of the book), lift each board off the covering cloth and place it
carefully face downward on its appropriate end-paper. This is merely
for the time being. Now take a large brush and apply glue all over the

126

cloth, working from the middle to the edges. Place the backing strip in position on the gluey surface, and press it down firmly. Take up the book and place the front board carefully on the guide-lines on the left-hand side of the material. The work should now look like Fig. 3, 3. Take the loose cloth on the right-hand side, and pull it over the board as indicated by the arrow in the diagram. Then, before the glue has a chance to harden, roll and press the work very well, including the back. It is best to cover the cloth with a clean piece of paper during this operation to help keep the surface clean. Now remove the book, tearing away the outer end-papers (to which you previously pasted the boards), and leaving the cover as in Fig. 3, 4. Turn the projecting flaps of the cloth over the edges of the boards—first the head, then the tail, and lastly the two fore-edges. Apply a little extra pressure on the corners. Then place in a dry, airy position to set thoroughly.

Cut a strip of muslin, linen, or calico about one inch shorter than the page depth and about three times the width of the back. Apply a liberal coating of glue to this, and place it on the back of the book, so that the overlapping pieces on the sides adhere to the outside end-papers (Fig. 3, 5). Now apply paste to the outside of the front end-paper, and, while it is still wet, place it carefully on to the left-hand board, which should project about $\frac{1}{8}$ in. all round. This end-paper will, of course, cover the edge of the turned-over flap of the covering material already stuck to the board. Now apply paste to the back of the book and to the back end-paper, and carefully pull the outside back cover over into position. Lastly place the complete book under a substantial weight and leave for about twenty-four hours.

The sewing press A method of sewing up a single-section or small multi-section book has already been described, but sewing is a little more involved for larger volumes. There are several methods. The one described here is an adaptation of the professional method of "ordinary" sewing, and a sewing press is desirable. A really practical press can easily be made at home on the lines shown in Fig. 4. Place all the sections in their proper order, and square them up. Place them in a press with the backs to the outside. On the backs measure $\frac{1}{2}$ in. from the head and

127

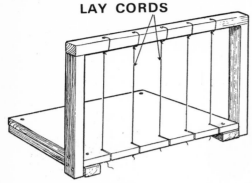

LAY CORDS

Figure 4. A simple sewing press, easily made at home.

$\frac{1}{2}$ in. from the tail, and mark both places with a pencil. Then, with the aid of a set-square, draw a vertical line right down the backs of the sections at these marks. Divide the space between these marks equally, and mark down the back in the same way. The number of divisions you have to make depends on the number of tapes or lay cords (see Fig. 4) you are going to use.

The lay cords are knotted into loops round the crossbar of the sewing press, and are tightened by means of keys inserted into the bed of the press. In the case of a home-made press the best method will suggest itself from the nature of the frame; tapes, for instance, can be attached with drawing-pins at top and bottom.

Lay cords must be of either very strong thread or string, and must be fixed on the press so that they exactly cover the vertical guide-lines on the backs of the sections.

Sawing in When you have marked up the backs of the sections, grip them firmly together and place them in a vice between two guard boards, with the backs uppermost. Cut a groove along each of the lines with a sharp, fine-toothed tenon saw (Fig. 5), just deep enough to reach the inside of the fold in the middle of each section. Now remove the sections, but keep them in

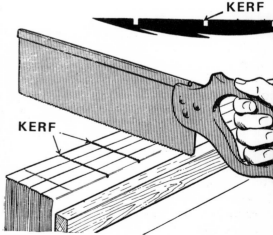

KERF

KERF

Figure 5. Sawing in.

(*above*) Books bound in leather will last through a lifetime of reading and handling. This book is being covered before the endpapers are pasted on.

(*right*) These Arcadia Press Limited Editions have fine bindings with Cockerell hand-marbled endpapers finished with gold-tooling. On the right are Solander boxes —in which all fine bindings should be kept.

Here are some particularly beautiful examples of books bound in a variety of materials with decorative gold blocking.

The Folio Society

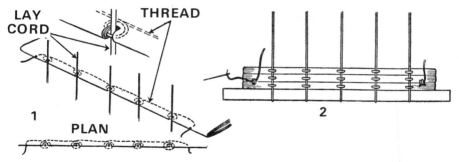

Figure 6. Stitching a large, multi-section book.

strict order of use and in a handy position to the sewing frame.

Stitching Place the first section face downward on the sewing frame with the grooves (or kerfs) fitting snugly round the lay cords. Using a stout darning needle, sew the sections horizontally one by one, adding a new section as each is finished. Sew the first section from right to left, continue the second section from left to right, and so on. You will see now that the kerfs allow you to sew horizontally round the lay cords very easily; they also keep most of the work invisible in the finished job. Use one continuous thread for sewing the entire book.

Fig. 6, 1 illustrates the path of the needle in making the stitches for the first section. First push the needle from the outside, at the extreme right-hand mark, to the middle of the fold of the inside (which you hold open with the left hand), leaving four or five inches of thread hanging loose. Carry the thread along the inside, and take it out at the second mark (which is crossed by the first lay cord). Take the thread round this lay cord, and back through the same hole to the inside. Carry the thread along the inside and out again at the third mark, round the second lay cord, and so on. When you reach the last mark of the first section your needle and thread will be on the outside of the section. Hold the first end of the thread (which was left hanging at the right) firmly with one hand, and then, with the finger and thumb of your free hand, pull the thread tight between each lay cord. Place the next section carefully on top of the first section, and pass the needle and thread from the outside to the inside, working in the reverse direction to that of the first section. On completing the second section pull the thread tight as before, and

129

press both sections tightly together. Continue in this way until you reach the last section. As the needle comes out of the last hole of each section, pass it horizontally round the thread and the top and bottom sections so that it forms a loop. Pass the needle through this loop, and pull tight to make a double knot. This is called a "kettle" stitch. When the needle emerges from its final hole, sew it through the thread of the lower section to form a knot (Fig. 6, 2), and cut the thread. Release the lay cords from the frame, and remove the book.

Rounding and backing Place the assembled sections on the bench or table with the back of the book away from you. Place your thumbs firmly on the middle of the fore-edges, and put the fingers of both hands on the top sections and drag them towards you. Turn the book over (with the

Figure 7. Rounding and backing, gluing up, lacing in and library-style binding.

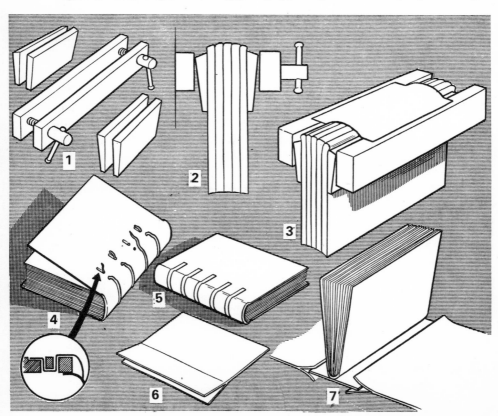

back away from you), and repeat the operation on the other side. This procedure is called rounding, and the object is to force the back of the book to take an even, smooth, and gentle curve. A little gentle assistance with a hammer will help.

Fig. 7, 1 shows how an ordinary bench vice can easily be adapted as a laying press and used to help in rounding. The wedges shown in the diagram have angled tops, as you can see from the side section in Fig. 7, 2; the wedges at the bottom of Fig. 7, 1 have flat tops and can be used for cutting.

After rounding, the book is ready for backing. Place it in the vice with the wedges on each side (Fig. 7, 2). The outside sections are bent outward above the wedges, so that a neat little groove is made along the edge of the outside sections into which the cover boards will fit. As the operation proceeds, tighten the vice and complete the rounding and backing by a gentle hammering in an outward direction. Never hammer on the top of the book.

Gluing up Hold the book firmly in the vice or laying press, and apply plenty of hot, fairly thin glue to the back, brushing it only in the up-and-down directions of the sections and well into the crevices. Smooth the surface with the fingers. Over the tacky surface place a piece of mull or muslin cut so that it will overlap the back of the book about 1 in. or a little more on each side, and is about 1 in. short of the head and tail (Fig. 7, 3). Rub the back of this well. Leave the work overnight to set before completing the binding.

Lacing in Lacing in disposes of the ends of the lay cords. If using light threads, lace them into knots round the other threads at the back of the sections or, alternatively, leave them loose and cover them with paste and end-papers when you attach the boards. But the professional method will be necessary if your lay cords are fairly thick.

Using a sharp knife, thin and taper the ends of the lay cords. Now pierce small holes in the board, one for each lay cord, in a line parallel to the back and about $\frac{1}{4}$ in. from it. Pierce another row of small holes parallel to the first row and $\frac{1}{4}$ to $\frac{1}{2}$ in. nearer the fore-edge. Cut shallow

131

V-shaped grooves to join these holes, first on the outside of the board from the back to each hole on the outside, and then on the back of the board from each hole in the first row to the corresponding hole in the second row. Coat each lay cord with paste, rub it between your finger and thumb to a fine point, and thread it from the back, outside the board and in the groove, through the first hole; carry it in the groove made in the back of the board, and bring it through the corresponding hole of the second row to the front again. Follow this procedure (Fig. 7, 4) for each lay cord in turn, and finally pull all the cords tight, fold back their ends, and, if necessary, place them in another little groove. Gently tap the lay cords with the hammer, then press the whole board.

Split boards Another method of binding, sometimes called the library style, involves the use of either two narrow pieces of strawboard or one fairly thick piece and one thin one. Paste and press these boards together and assemble them as shown in Fig. 7, 5-7. Sew the book on to tapes, and then cut, round, and back it in the manner already described. Prepare the " split " boards, leaving a strip about $1\frac{1}{2}$ in. wide not pasted on the back edge. Fold back the waste sheets of end-paper, and glue them over the tapes; or, alternatively, cut both the end-papers and the tapes down to the width of the split. Apply a liberal coating of glue to the inside of the split, insert the tapes, press tightly, and leave to set under pressure.

In the real library style the boards are taped about $\frac{1}{8}$ in. away from the joint to make what is called a French groove, which allows for the thick covering usually used for the style.

Binding styles There are four main types of book bindings, each with many variations. They are:
1 Cased binding. This is the most common and the cheapest method, and the one already described. The covering is usually some form of book cloth.
2 Quarter binding. This is substantially the same as a cased binding, with the notable exception that the back (and the back only) is of leather.
3 Half binding. In addition to the leather back of the quarter binding, the half binding has leather corners (four in all). Fig. 8 shows the

132

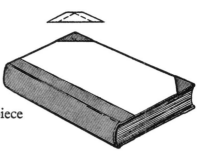

Figure 8. Leather-backed half-binding.

pattern required for the leather corner and
its appearance when completed.

4 Full binding. This is made from a single piece
of leather.

Leather bindings   Morocco is the best leather, but calf is more popular
because it is easier to tool.   Pigskin tends to be too solid and hard for the
amateur.   Sheepskin is the least expensive, and is recommended for the
beginner to practise on.   Skivers are not recommended.

Full leather bindings need special care, and it is wise to have some
practical instruction at your local technical school.   An allowance has to
be made for the turn-in if edge-paring is necessary, and in which the
leather has to be thinned down all round the edges, and there is also
specialized work for raised bands, decorations, and tooling.

Finishing   You can apply your title to the simpler bindings either by
hand-lettered " plates " or sometimes by lettering directly on to the cloth.

Leather bindings can, of course, be polished, and are usually given
a final pressing.   Cloth bindings, when otherwise complete, can be given
a coat of varnish.   The very quick-drying bookbinders' varnish is the
best for this purpose.   Apply it with a wad of cotton-wool.

These instructions should enable you to bind competently many types
of books in a wide variety of styles and materials.   But an account as
short as this can only introduce you to the fascinating craft of bookbinding;
if you want to produce really fine bindings using expensive leathers, you
are strongly recommended to take a course in the subject at a technical
or art school.

Pewterwork

Pewter has long been known to the craftsman. It was certainly used by the Romans and possibly by such ancient peoples as the Chinese and the Chaldeans before them. In the past the use of pewter has been widely varied: altar vessels, drinking tankards, furniture decoration, jewellery, and plates have all been made with this lovely material, for until quite recently pewter was frequently employed when gold or silver were out of the question due to their cost. During the sixteenth, seventeenth, and eighteenth centuries, pewterworkers were producing work of very great beauty and it was only with the coming of the Victorians that its use began to decline. Recently, however, its popularity has increased again, and small wonder, for it is soft, easier to work than most metals, and quite lovely things can be made with it by the amateur with only limited time and money.

Materials and tools   Pewter is an alloy of tin and lead. There are several grades and qualities, and in the best kind of pewter the proportion of tin is 95 per cent. It is bought in sheets of ·006 to ·008 of an inch in thickness, and a roll of medium-thick pewter of twelve inches width costs about ten shillings a foot. Because it is so easily dented and marked it must be very carefully protected and stored. For modelled pewterwork a filler is needed to protect the relief portions from being pressed out of shape. Barbola paste or the cheaper wallart may be used. Other essential materials include grease-remover, pewter patina (oxidizing agent), and adhesives (liquid glue and cement).

Tools may be of either metal or especially toughened glass, which has the advantage of being less likely to scratch or pierce the material in working. The main tools are illustrated in Fig. 1. They are: a double ball tool (1), a Dresden tool (2), a punch (3), a straight tracer and

134

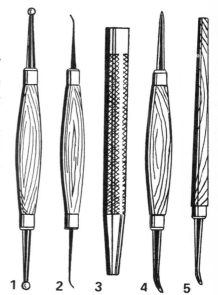

Figure 1. Pewterwork tools.

modeller (4), and a bent tracer (5). These are the same tools that are used for modelling leather. None of them costs more than about ten shillings. Other essentials are a light hammer or mallet to use with the punch, a pair of curved scissors, a nail file, and a soft duster or felt pad.

Any table-top or bench may be used for working pewter—provided that the surface is clean and smooth and free from anything that might cause scratches or dents. If the surface is rough this can easily be put right by covering it with a piece of linoleum or similar material.

Transferring the design The next things to explore are the various techniques of working pewter and to learn how to handle the specialized tools. To do this either practise on a scrap piece of pewter, or, better still, make a simple article such as a small box-lid.

Whilst it is possible to buy printed designs to decorate the things you make, it is far more interesting and instructive to copy someone else's designs in pewter—especially those of a real craftsman—until you have developed a feeling for designing in the metal. But in either case the first step is to make a copy of the design on tracing paper. Leave out small details, which you can put in free-hand after modelling. Now place the tracing on the bright side of the pewter and hold it in position with a strip of adhesive tape along one side only, or with a bulldog clip, as in Fig 2, 1. You can then inspect the pewter as you go along.

The next step is to transfer the outline on to the pewter, and you do this very lightly with a straight tracer. Hold the tool like a pen or pencil, as in Fig. 2, 2. Always draw it along—don't push it—and use only enough pressure to make the lightest possible outline on the pewter. In order to avoid making too much of an impression you should use a very thin felt supporting pad or even a sheet of cardboard between the pewter and the surface of the base.

135

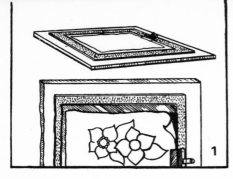

Modelling Lift up the tracing paper to check that all the main lines have been transferred. Then remove the paper, place the pewter on a thicker (but not too thick) supporting pad, and impress the outline into the metal.

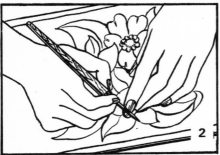

For this you need a bent tracer, which should also be held like a pencil or pen —between the thumb and first two fingers—with the bent end pointing to the left. Place your left index finger a little above the bend, and use it to control the pressure and guide the stroke, as shown in Fig. 2, 3. Always work from left to right, again draw the tool away from its point rather than pushing it into the line of work. The appearance of the finished article depends largely on this stage, and it is worth while to practise with the bent tracer until all your strokes are smooth, clean, and firm. Care and accuracy are not quite enough: for the best results you need to be bold, too.

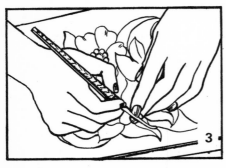

Now turn the pewter over, so that the face or shiny side is underneath. Then, with the same supporting pad, impress a second outline with the bent tracer on the dull side of the metal. Make this outline inside and about two millimetres distant from the first line —which, of course, appears now as

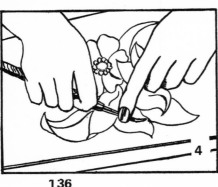

Figure 2. The basic technique for making a pewterwork article.

136

a ridge. The second line will show as a ridge on the bright side of the pewter, and its purpose is to give the design a raised edge. The method of making the outline and the amount of pressure should be exactly the same.

Turn the metal over again, inspect the new outline, and then go over the first outline again with a bent tracer, to make a clean, well-defined edge.

For low-relief work this may be all the modelling that has to be done; except, of course, for putting in any smaller lines or other details in the design that you did not include in the tracing. This done, proceed with the filling and other finishing processes described below.

High-relief modelling For high-relief work further modelling is required. To begin with you may have to press the background flat. To do this, keep the pewter face-side up, and support it on a firm, flat surface, then press down the area round the design with either your fingers or a modelling tool covered with soft cloth. Turn the work over again, on to a thick, soft pad of duster or felt, and press out the relief. Use a modelling tool for this. It should be held differently from the tracer—not like a pen or pencil, but gripped lightly between the thumb and fingers so that it is almost horizontal, as in Fig. 2, 4.

The outer curve of the end of the tool should rest lightly on the pewter, with the tip pointing upward and clear of the metal. Again control the amount of pressure with your left index finger, placing it on the inner curve of the blade. Work the tool gently and smoothly from side to side, not from back to front.

Work slowly and gradually, frequently stopping and turning the pewter over to inspect the other side. Whenever necessary, press the background flat with your fingers. Take care not to model too near the outline, or you may cause the edge to bulge and spoil the clearness of the design. If, when you inspect the other side, you find any such bulges, rub them out carefully with your fingers, supporting the metal with a smooth flat surface.

During this part of the modelling process you may need to use the ball or Dresden tool, which is designed for raising hollowed-out areas. Hold it like a pencil, and raise small round bumps either by a gentle circular movement or simply by pressing. Outline them on the other (face) side with the straight tracer.

When the metal has been raised sufficiently, take the bent tracer and, working on the dull side, put in the lines and other details that you left out of your tracing of the original design. Then turn the pewter right side up, and press down the background until it is completely flat. If you wish to produce a dotted background, which helps to throw the design into greater relief, go over it carefully with a tooling punch. The point of the straight tracer can be used instead of the tooling punch.

Finishing The first of the finishing processes is filling the raised parts to prevent dents or other damage. Barbola paste is the easiest to use, and especially suitable when the surface of the mount is curved and the pewter therefore has to be mounted before the filling has hardened. When the mount is flat, the filling should be allowed to set hard, and all superfluous matter taken away with grease-remover before the mounting.

Grease-remover should be applied on a piece of wet cotton wool and rubbed vigorously over the whole face of the pewter to remove all traces of dirt and grease. Afterwards wash with cold water, and then, if you want a bright finish, rub over with metal polish. After the polishing, wash again in cold water and dry. If you want a matt finish, instead of metal polish rub the pewter with a little pumice powder on damp cotton wool, then wash and dry and varnish. For an antique finish use pewter petina as an oxidizing agent.

Things to make in pewter Brooches and jewellery, box tops and lids, bowls, tankards, ash-trays, book-ends, small plaques, plates, and name-plates are some of the many things that the skilled pewterworker can make with great beauty.

A useful and simple exercise to begin with would be to make yourself a pair of cuff-links such as those shown in Fig. 3. Unless you want to undertake the entire job, which is not easy, it is a good idea to purchase a pair of ready-made cuff-link bases which are quite reasonable. Then you

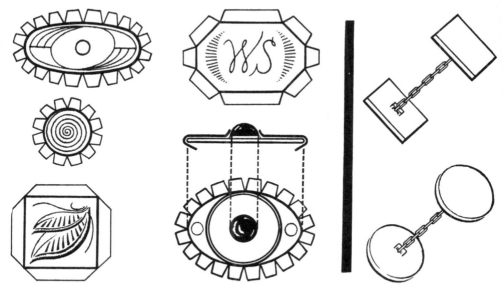

Figure 3. Left: five designs for pewterwork cuff-links showing the types of flanges to keep the facing in place over the base. Also shown is the method for incorporating a stone. Right: two pairs of cuff-link bases.

can concentrate all your effort on the making of the pewterwork covering. Fig. 3 shows a pair of bases and you can see that it would not be difficult to make the caps of pewter, decorated on the faces, to fit them. The caps in each case are fitted with small flanges which are folded under the base and cemented to hold the two parts firmly together. While most of the designs shown can be modelled as described above, one of the designs allows for a small stone. These can be obtained in a number of colours and sizes and would give a rather artistic effect to the work. Stones are fitted as follows: trace a circle or oval slightly smaller than the size of the stone on to the pewter. Then transfer any design that is to surround the stone. With this done, the hole should be cut *making sure* that it is smaller than the stone. This is to provide a collar to keep the stone firmly in place. See Fig. 4. If a very small stone is being used, the hole can probably be cut with a small punch. With a larger stone, first punch a small hole in the centre and then cut away the surplus metal with a sharp knife or scissors. When any modelling necessary has been

139

Figure 4. Showing how a gem stone is inset.

completed, the collar for the stone should be raised, but *not* before. Now stick the stone to the base and do the rest of the assembling. As stones are made from a variety of materials, you should find out what kind of adhesive to use when buying the stone.

Coloured stones can be used for all manner of pewterwork and in most cases the method of attaching them is the same as described here.

Covering a box with pewterwork When you have gained some experience in handling pewter, you will certainly want to attempt something larger and rather more complicated. Covering a box or casket with pewter will provide plenty of opportunities for exercising your skill and feeling for design, although it is by no means a difficult job. Fig. 5 shows the stages and plans for making the pewter shell, and you can either make the box yourself or purchase it ready-made.

The most important point to watch is that the flaps which bend underneath to keep the lid in position may well make the lid too tight to fit without strain. This increased thickness can be allowed for by sanding down the wooden flanges accordingly. An alternative to folding the metal beneath the lid is to fix the pewter to the sides of the lid with small panel-pins or rivets.

Work in this order:

1 If hinged, remove lid.

2 Make the covering for the lid. First, cut out a paper pattern (on the lines shown in Fig. 5, 1) with the utmost care and fold it over the lid in the same way that the metal will be used. It is vital to take into account that the paper is considerably thinner than the metal. This will affect

140

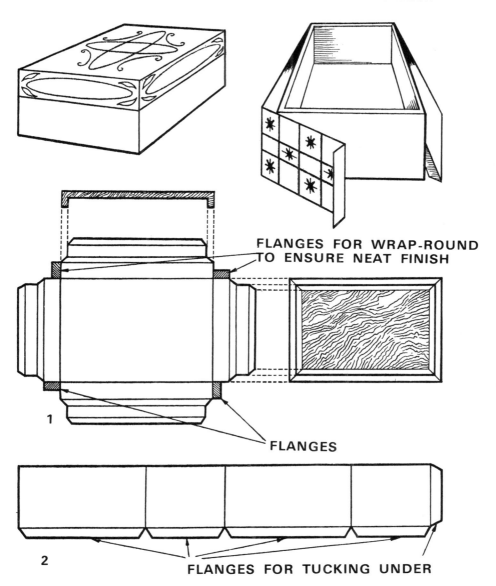

Pewterwork box

FLANGES FOR WRAP-ROUND
TO ENSURE NEAT FINISH

1

FLANGES

2

FLANGES FOR TUCKING UNDER

Figure 5. Plans for covering a wooden box with pewter.

folds, etc. To avoid the flanges for the sides of the lid showing through the shell, a slight recess can be sanded in the wood of the lid to take these flanges.

3 Cut out the metal for the lid and transfer the design.

4 Model the design.

5 If used, cut out the metal for the lining (it should be thinner than that used for the lid) to cover the inside of the lid exactly. Cement, and press with a cloth to obtain a close fit.

6 Cement and pin the pewter for the top and sides of the lid.

7 If the sides of the box are to be covered in metal, prepare the pewter in the same way as the lid. The sides should be cut in one long strip as Fig. 5, 2. Alternatively, the wood can be left plain and polished or stained.

8 Cement and pin the sides.

9 Polish the metal in the usual way.

The pewterwork techniques described in this chapter are suitable for anyone making a beginning in the craft. To progress further you will have to refer to books on advanced technique, or better still, take a course in pewterwork.

**Figure 6.   Another design for a pewterwork box
using stones set in the side.**

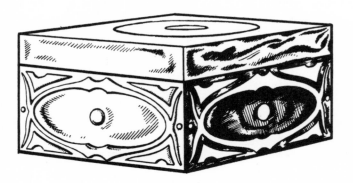

Leatherwork

Although leatherwork is a more expensive craft than most of those described in this book, it is one that will give the young craftworker the opportunity of showing considerable skill in making articles that are a pleasure to see and use. Unfortunately, the best quality leathers are not cheap, but as it will be some time before your skill has advanced sufficiently to be able to get the best use from them, the cheaper leathers, synthetic hides and plastic leather cloths are adequate and reasonable enough for practice and ordinary work.

Tools Leatherwork requires a number of specialized tools and fittings, all of which cost money. The beginner should, therefore, buy only those tools that are absolutely necessary for the work in hand, and then add other items from time to time as they are needed. Most of the tools required are suitable only for leatherwork, although some are useful also for working with some plastic materials and pewter.

The following list comprises the essential tools and equipment needed for ordinary work. Most of them are illustrated in Fig. I.

Scissors; a sharp cutting knife; a metal straight-edge (or a rule); a light hammer; a six-way revolving punch; stitch-markers; a thonging punch; ordinary sewing needles; strong thread; brown paper; paste and vegetable glues.

A sheet of zinc or thick glass makes an admirable cutting board, although mill-board will make an excellent alternative. Various stains may be needed for finishing. You will note that there are two kinds of adhesive. The paste is used mainly for sticking linings.

A few extra tools will be required for leather modelling. These include a tracing tool; a broad-ended modeller; and a double-ended Dresden tool. Matting tools can be added as required and effective pattern

143

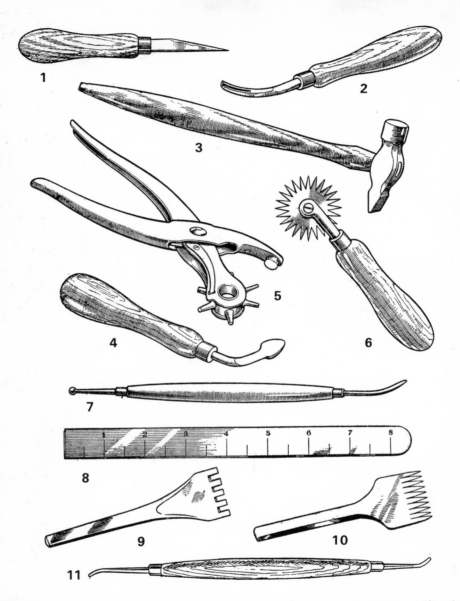

Figure 1. Leatherwork tools: 1, knife; 2, curved modeller; 3, hammer; 4, broad modeller; 5, six-way revolving punch; 6, revolving stitch-spacer; 7, straight tracer and medium modeller; 8, non-slip metal ruler; 9, slit punch for thonging; 10, stitch-marker tool; 11, Dresden tool.

144

Removing the iron mould from the top half of a cast of a pewter vase.

Tin Research Institute

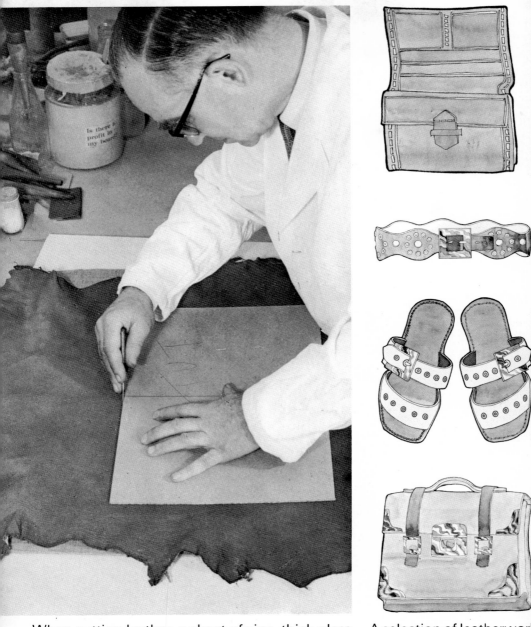

When cutting leather, a sheet of zinc, thick glass or millboard should be used as a cutting board.

A selection of leatherwor[k] See how punched an[d] eyeletted holes can for[m] attractive decoration.

punches can easily be made from brass screws, as will be described later. One or two special tools are required for fitting some of the accessories, such as press-buttons.

Materials Practically all the leather used for "soft" leatherwork is made from the skins of sheep, goats, or calves. Sheepskin is relatively cheap and perhaps the most popular material. It is sold both in its natural form and stamped by machine (and suitably coloured) to resemble other kinds of skin such as crocodile, alligator, lizard, python and morocco. Most of the skins sold for home craftwork under these and similar names are, in fact, sheepskins.

Sheepskins appear in many forms. When it is split, the under-skin becomes chamois and the outer-skin (which is of poorer quality) is called skivers. Suède leather is made from either sheepskin or goatskin ground to a smooth finish. It is a pleasant, soft and easily worked material that is particularly suitable for elementary work. "Velvet Persians" have a fine, soft, velvety texture not unlike suède; "lacing Persians" are much the same but are thinner, and are therefore useful for gussets and thongs. One of the best sheepskins on which to start modelling is Basil. It is an undyed skin which retains its natural grain, and although it will "take" some coloured inks it does not take stains so well.

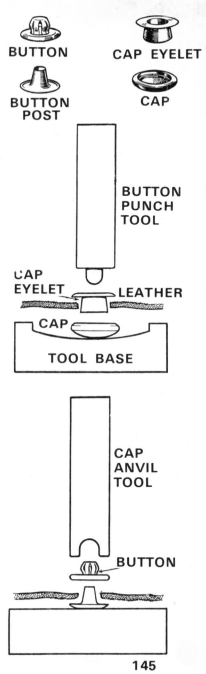

Figure 2. **Tools for fixing press-studs.**

145

Kinds of leather

Real morocco is a goatskin with a fine grained surface and is rather expensive. It should not be confused with imitation morocco, which is merely sheepskin finished with an imitation surface. Calf leathers are the best for modelling work; "natural calf" is excellent for practice work; "brown English calf" is good for producing an "antique" finish, and "natural English calf" is a high quality, all-purpose leather.

Synthetic hides and plastic leather cloths such as P.V.C. are easy to obtain from nearly any craft-goods supplier. These materials are comparatively cheap and are admirable for practising the various techniques. Many small articles normally made with leather can, and frequently are, made with these substitute materials, but they are never as pleasant to look at or handle as real leather, nor are they as durable. Plastic thonging can be bought in various thicknesses and finishes, and can be used with the synthetic hides for the cheaper types of articles. For the better class of work it is a good idea to buy leather thongs already cut to the width you want, because leather is difficult to cut evenly. When you buy a leather thong in this way, choose one with a natural finish so that it can be stained to harmonize with the rest of the work.

Before actually starting on leatherwork, get thoroughly used to the tools and their uses. One of the best ways to do this is to buy a few pieces of poor-quality hides which are called "rejects" and are sold very cheaply.

Fitments for leatherwork Various fitments and accessories play an important part in leatherwork. They can be bought in a very wide range of sizes, styles, and colours. The most important are press-studs, eyelets, domes, clasps, handle loops and handbag frames. There are many variations of these. Others include fitments for key-cases, metal frames to fit inside leather cigarette-cases, plain or fancy bag "pullers", and zip-fasteners of different weights and lengths.

Press-studs Press-studs are probably the most important members of the "fittings family". They are used to button-up gloves, purses, wallets, etc. One complete press-stud is made up of four parts, which are illustrated (with the method of fitting) in Fig. 2. The top half is made up of the cap which fits over the cap eyelet after a piece of material has been placed between the two pieces. Similarly, for the lower half the button fits over the button post, with another piece of material between. When assembled in this way, the parts form the common press-stud fastening used in most types of gloves.

The stud pieces are fitted together with the aid of two special tools (shown in section in Fig. 2). The button punch has a projection which is pressed into the inside recess of the inverted cap eyelet, forcing it into the cap. The cap anvil has a recess which fits over the button and forces it down over the button-post. The different shapes of the bases in Fig. 2 are, of course, part of the tool set.

Unfortunately, stud-fitting tools can only be used to fit press-studs of one particular size. Every different size of stud needs a new pair of tools. This is an important point to remember when you are buying one.

Attaching the stud is quite simple. Punch a hole, just large enough to take the projection on the stud, on the precise position marked on the pattern. Fit the stud cap together first, and then the button. Hold the tools perfectly upright while you are pressing the parts together. Give the top of the tool a slight tap with the hammer if necessary.

Eyelets Metal eyelets are like the lace-holes in shoes and have many useful purposes in leatherwork. The single eyelet has a smooth base like a washer with a tiny "cylinder" fitting above the hole. The double-sail eyelet consists of two parts, one fitting inside the other, the tubular "cylinder" being the hole through which a lace can be passed. These eyelets are, in fact, very much like tubular rivets.

Eyelets are fitted with an eyelet

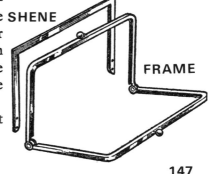

Figure 3. Handbag frame and shene.

147

fixing tool, which consists of a small anvil and punch and is used in much the same way as the press-stud tools.

Domes   Domes are small metal fittings shaped like inverted mushrooms, which are attached to the bottoms of many larger bags.   They serve partly as a protection to the bag both from normal wear and from standing on the wet ground, as they protrude from the surrounding surface. The "stalk" of the mushroom shape consists of two prongs, and you fit the dome by pushing these prongs through suitably punched holes. When you have thus got the dome in position on the outside of the material, bend the two prongs back sharply until they lie flat on the surrounding material on the inside.   When using domes on the bottom of a bag it is advisable to insert card or some other stiffener for reinforcement. Larger domes are supplied with metal back-plates so that the domes will not tear out easily.

Clasps   The clapette is the most popular and fashionable clasp for handbags, and can be obtained in a wide variety of plain or ornamental designs, with all kinds of finishes and in many sizes.   Most clasps are easily fitted with the aid of an eyelet or rivet punch.   The old twin-knob bag-and-purse clasp can still be obtained from some suppliers.

Handle loops and ends   Practically every kind of handbag or carrying bag has either a handle or a shoulder-strap, and a fitting is needed to link the handle securely to the bag itself.   The simplest and most familiar fitting is the Deering (shaped like the letter D).   It is easy to attach it to the bag.   Cut a short strip of leather of slightly narrower width than the straight bar of the D, and double this strip round the bar.   Stitch through the double thickness right across the leather, close and parallel to the bar, which is thus securely held by a leather collar. You can cut this leather strip to some form of design if you wish.   Finally stitch the strip to the bag.

Handbag frames   A handbag frame comprises a hinged outer frame (the visible part of the finished bag) and a pair of shenes.   The shene is a three-sided piece of metal shaped like an inverted U.   You insert the

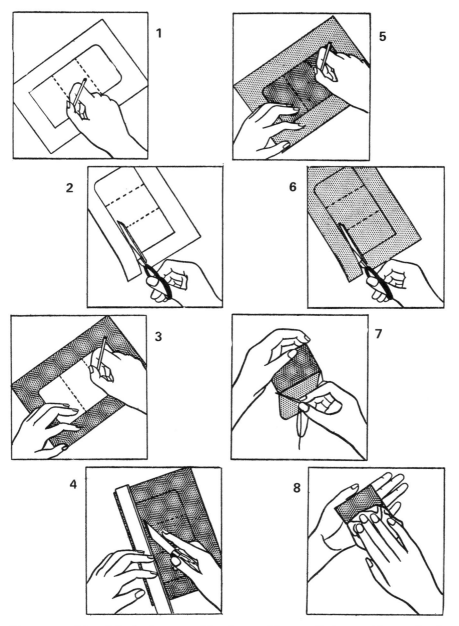

Figure 4. The eight basic steps of leatherworking applied to making a simple purse.

top edge strip of leather and the gussets into this U, which you then gently and evenly tap all round with a mallet, so that the leather is gripped inside the U (see Fig. 3). When you attach shenes to each side of the frame, place them in the hollowed-out portion of the frame, fit properly, and then rivet them into the frame with the rivets and holes provided.

SIMPLE LEATHERWORK

The order of operations for all simple leatherwork is as follows (see Fig. 4):

1 Plan the pattern and mark out on paper.
2 Cut out the paper pattern.
3 Group and mark the pattern on the skin.
4 Cut out pattern.
5 Lay skin over lining and mark.
6 Cut out lining.
7 Join up and assemble.
8 Stain and polish.

The pattern Never start on a piece of leatherwork without first drawing a pattern. Take as much care with this work as with the actual material. Draw the lines with a pencil, ruler and, if necessary, compasses. When you have finished this exact pattern drawing, check it again and then again. When you are sure it is absolutely correct, cut each piece out with the greatest of care. You can cut the straight lines with a razor blade (or sharp knife) and rule, but you must cut the curves with scissors.

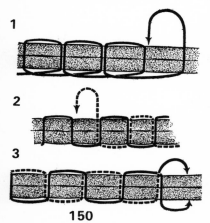

Now set the paper pattern on to the skin in the most economical positions, first placing the inner (or flesh) side of the hide face downward. Hold very firmly, and carefully mark the outlines in pencil. After a little experience you will be able to do the marking with the tracing tool. When you have marked all parts of the pattern on the skin, cut them out, using the sharp cutting knife and steel

Figure 5. Types of leather stitching.

straight-edge for the straight lines and sharp scissors for curves.

Lining Articles made with calf skin are usually lined with a skiver of a colour to tone or contrast with the outer surface. After cutting the skiver to the required size, cover the inner surface of the calfskin with paste, taking care that you leave no lumps of paste on the skiver. Then apply the skiver, press firmly to eliminate any air bubbles, and leave under pressure until thoroughly set.

Joining up You can join up the pieces of the leather pattern either by machine-sewing or hand-sewing or by thonging. Thonging is easy and therefore one of the most popular methods but can never compare with the neat appearance of good hand-stitching.

Thonging The beginner will find it best to buy thonging that is already cut. Thonging is simply a process of lacing (in one of several ways) through holes that have been cut or punched beforehand. The pronged, forklike type of punch is best where the thonging is thin and a row of slits is preferred. The six-way revolving punch is the ideal tool for making round holes suitable for broader thongings. Articles to be thonged should have rounded corners, as it is not easy to work round square corners.

To prepare for thonging mark a guide line on the surface of the leather, but not too close to the edge. The width of your margin will depend on the article and its size. Space and mark off the holes, arranging for a hole to come in each corner; do the corner holes first. The usual distance between holes is $\frac{1}{4}$ in.

About two and a half times the length of the edges to be thonged will represent the length of thonging required. For small articles one length will usually be enough, but for larger articles you will have to join separate pieces of thonging. When joining two ends of thonging together, "skive" or thin each end and then touch it lightly with the adhesive, press, and hold firmly together until set. To start thonging, skive one end of the thonging and glue it between the two pieces near the starting point. You can bring endings through the last hole and then thin and stick them between the two pieces.

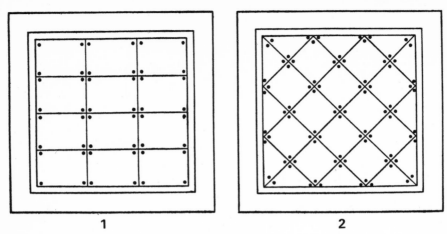

Figure 6. Designs made with punched patterns.

Sewing   Hand-sewing and stitching are not so difficult as it is often supposed. You mark the stitch holes with the revolving stitch-maker, and punch the tiny holes through with a stitch punch or awl. The thread can be of either a matching or contrasting shade to the leather. The three main kinds of leather-stitching all give a neat and unbroken line. The three types are illustrated in Fig. 5 which also shows the method of sewing. The saddle stitch (Fig. 5, 3), in which two needles are used, is the best.

Staining   Leather may be coloured or toned either with stain or by dyeing. Staining is the better method for the beginner. Not all leatherwork needs stain or colour. In any case, you should not begin staining until every bit of the earlier work is completed.

Polishing   A good wax polish is usually used for calfskin. Rub the surface well with a clean dry cloth before application. Almost any good wax furniture polish, and *some* shoe polishes, are suitable.

Decorative work in leather

Leather is a beautiful material in itself, and almost invariably looks better with too little decoration rather than with too much. Do not try to gild the lily. Think rather in terms of the minimum of decoration you can use.

152

A charming leather inlay effect is easily obtained with leather appliqué. The design must, as always, be original and suitable for the particular article. Monograms, stylized scroll, and floral forms can all look attractive. Draw the design very carefully on thin leather, and then cut it out cleanly and accurately with sharp scissors. Paste the underside well, and allow it to get tacky. Then attach it to the ground leather, back on front, and hold it down under pressure. When it has set well, work over the outline with the modelling tool. You can get a reverse, or inlay, effect in a similar way by cutting a design out of a piece of leather so that it looks just like a stencil. Paste this to the main piece of leather in the same way as for the appliqué. When the paste has set thoroughly, press all the edges of the cut-out into the ground surface with the rounded modelling tool. Both these methods of decoration look very well when worked in two harmonizing shades of leather.

Modelling and tooling Modelling is working an embossed or low-relief design in the surface of the actual leather. Tooling is making an outline design in the surface of the leather with modelling tools and tooling punches. Many useful and attractive designs can be built up by using a combination of these punches (as in Fig. 6). You can buy punches with a design already cut on the metal surface, but you can also make punches at home by screwing a flat brass screw into a wooden holder and then filing a simple design on the top of the screw. Work out the pattern on squared paper beforehand, and then test it by using the punch and an inking pad just as you would a rubber stamp. Use firm, fine-grained leathers for modelled decoration; the best are calfskin, cow-hide and sheepskin. Patterned surfaces are unsuitable. Modelling-leather is usually prepared, and is very receptive to impressions, especially when moistened.

Transferring the design When you have prepared your design, carefully draw it on strong tracing paper. Then place the leather on a firm, smooth surface, lay the tracing over it and secure it in position in such a manner that parts can be lifted for inspection during the tracing. You can use

Figure 7. Handling the modelling tool.

Sinking the designs

paper or other clips fastened over cardboard guards for this purpose but make sure they don't mark the leather. If the leather is firm or fairly thick, moisten it all over slightly before tracing. Using either a hard pencil or the special tracing tool, trace the outline firmly and evenly and with clean lines, pressing just firm enough to leave a light, line impression to guide the modelling tools.

Sinking the design Moisten the complete design with a damp sponge. Using the broad end of the double-ended tool, press down the leather all round the traced outline, firmly and evenly, so that the border is slightly raised. Now pull the tool over the leather, working with the grain: never push it hard or into the surface. Hold the tool rather like a pencil, with the handle tilted in front of the point and towards the line being worked (as in Fig. 7). It is best to apply pressure by degrees, working over the same ground to ensure a smooth, even background with the outline clearly indicated. When you have completed the outline, sink the surrounding spaces by going over them with a sideways pressure of the modelling tool.

Matting The sunken background surrounding the relief design can either be left plain (and subsequently polished), or, for greater contrast, matted, pricked or stippled, although this must be done with discretion. Many workers prefer to leave backgrounds plain.

Matting is best done with special matt punches, which are held vertically over the work and very lightly tapped with a mallet or hammer. Be careful to ensure that the punch impressions do not overlap, or you will get an ugly blemish that cannot be removed. Pricking and stippling consists merely of light stabbing

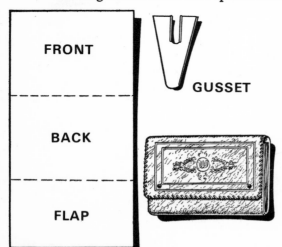

Figure 8. The pattern for a simple purse. A much neater effect is obtained by stitching rather than thonging.

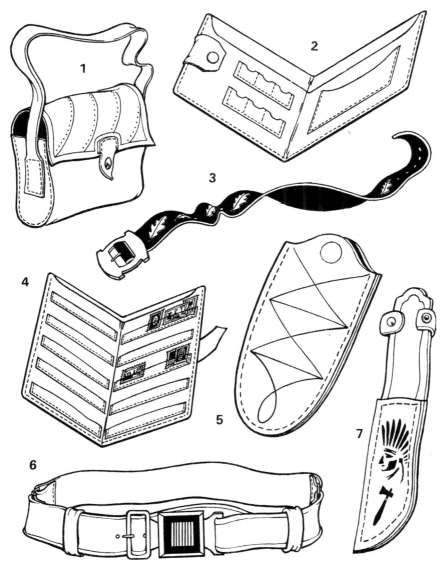

Figure 9. Suggestions for articles to make in leather: 1, girl's handbag; 2, wallet; 3, girl's belt; 4, stamp case (with transparent plastic pockets); 5, spectacle case; 6, hiker's belt; 7, scout knife sheath.

155

with any tool that will leave an even, consistent impression on the surface. A needle, tracing tool, knitting needle or skewer will serve admirably.

High-relief modelling For high-relief modelling (such as is often used for modelling floral patterns) you prepare the preliminary surface modelling in the manner already described. Then you turn the leather over, protecting the front surface contours by placing the leather face-down on a soft surface, such as modelling-clay or wax, with a sheet of pliable paper between. Alternatively you can hold it against your free hand. The design on the face of the leather should be visible from the under-side. Now you model the lines or areas to be raised from the under-side with the ball tool, or, for an extra-bold relief, with rounded punches and a hammer. When you have finished modelling from the under-side, fill the raised parts with a mixture of cotton-wool and paste, and attach the lining. Then place the work right side up, and complete the modelling and re-touching.

Things to make in leather
Glove-making and slipper-making are two highly specialized branches of leatherwork requiring more complicated treatment that can be described here. The techniques described above, however, should enable you to plan and make a wide variety of attractive and useful leather articles, including bookmarks, pochettes, stamp-cases, lanyards, belts; spectacle, scissors, and knife-cases; ticket-holders, photo-frames, album covers, comb-cases, table-napkin rings, blotters, tobacco pouches, wallets, dress accessories, book-covers and stationery cases. Designs for some of these are shown in Fig. 9.

Designs for modelling The basic principles of design are: 1 that it should be pleasing; 2 that should be suitable for its purpose; 3 that it should be as simple as possible—that is, not overworked; and 4 that it should have symmetry and balance. Monograms are probably the simplest of all modelling forms to work.

156

INDEX

Index